THE
LITURGICAL
MINISTRY
SERIES

GUIDE FOR LECTORS

Virginia Meagher
Paul Turner

LTP

LITURGY
TRAINING
PUBLICATIONS

Nihil Obstat
Reverend Brian J. Fischer
Censor Deputatus
November 22, 2006

Imprimatur
Reverend John F. Canary, STL, DMIN
Vicar General
Archdiocese of Chicago
November 27, 2006

In the beginning was the Word,
*   and the Word was with God,*
*   and the Word was God.*
He was in the beginning with God.
All things came to be through him,
*   and without him nothing came to be.*
What came to be through him was life,
*   and this life was the light of the human race;*
the light shines in the darkness,
*   and the darkness has not overcome it.*

—John 1:1–5

Table of Contents

Preface

The Spirit of the Lord is upon me,
because he has anointed me
to bring glad tidings to the poor.
He has sent me to proclaim liberty to captives
and recovery of sight to the blind,
to let the oppressed go free,
and to proclaim a year acceptable to the Lord.
—*Luke 4:18–19*

"The Spirit of the Lord is upon me,"[1] Jesus read. He was reading out loud in front of his boyhood neighbors at a synagogue service one Sabbath. Now he was an adult. "The Spirit of the Lord . . . has anointed me,"[2] he continued. People started to pay a little more attention.

Jesus had grown up as any child did. He lived at home. He had friends. He played in the streets. He washed his hands before dinner. The neighbors watched his parents age, and they witnessed his growth in wisdom and grace. One day he left on a spiritual quest. He approached John the Baptist, a charismatic figure with a band of disciples. Jesus surprised John by asking to be baptized, and John agreed. Coming up from the waters, he walked into the desert, where he spent 40 days fasting, praying, and overcoming temptation. Now it was time to go to work.

"The Spirit of the Lord . . . has anointed me / to bring glad tidings to the poor,"[3] Jesus read. People listened even more closely. They had been talking about him ever since he returned to Galilee.

Jesus had already preached in nearby towns, but now he was back home in Nazareth. He was walking the streets of his old neighborhood, seeing familiar faces and summoning up memories. This particular day was the Sabbath. He did something he was accustomed to do: he showed up at the synagogue. His neighbors were excited to see him there. They knew of his growing reputation as a spiritual leader, so they asked him to do what he used to do: read the scripture for the day.

So here is Jesus—the Word of God made flesh. An attendant reaches over and hands him the word of God on parchment. Jesus picks up the scroll. He unfurls it. He finds the passage he wants. He reads with a voice that would rivet individuals and large throngs: "The Spirit of the Lord is upon me, / because he has anointed me / to bring glad tidings to the poor."[4]

He improvises. He is reading Isaiah 61:1–3, but he interpolates some of Isaiah 58:6, rearranges parts, and adds a thought. He seems to have something very specific in mind. Jesus reads: "He has sent me to proclaim liberty to captives / and recovery of sight to the blind, / to let the oppressed go free, / and to proclaim a year acceptable to the Lord."[5]

His words caught the attention of everyone in the room. They no longer looked at the wall, their sandals, the ceiling, or the floor. They all turned their eyes toward Jesus. Something was happening. They were listening to the word of God read by the Word of God. They were listening to God.

The message was unmistakable. Hundreds of years prior, through the mouth of Isaiah, God had promised a new kind of liberation; now that promise was being heard—and fulfilled—in their midst.

After reading these few words, Jesus rolled up the scroll, handed it back to the attendant, and took his seat. The worshippers all stared at him. His words hung like humidity in the room.

Then he gave one of the shortest and most powerful homilies ever: "Today this scripture passage is fulfilled in your hearing."[6]

This story took place in a remote synagogue long ago, but it still transmits an eternal message about who Jesus is, and what the word of God is.

"The word of God is living and effective," the letter to the Hebrews says, "sharper than any two-edged sword, penetrating even between soul and spirit, joints and marrow, and able to discern reflections and thoughts of the heart."[7]

When we pick up the word of God, we hold a powerful tool.

The story of Jesus in the synagogue also says something about the role of the lector. As a lector, Jesus had made the word of God part of his life. He was familiar with the scriptures. He had absorbed their thoughts into his own.

Jesus was a member of a community. People knew him as a child, and had followed his interests as an adult. Those who attended the synagogue service knew who he was as a person, and also as a minister. They knew he was a lector.

The synagogue service made space for the word of God. It relied not just on the written word, but also on the spoken word. Worship included the reading of God's word out loud.

The synagogue lector fulfilled this role in relationship with others. As a lector, Jesus interacted with one other minister, the attendant who handed him the scroll and later took it back. It seems like a small matter, but Jesus had to know the responsibilities of others in order properly to fulfill his own.

When Jesus finally proclaimed the reading, he spoke with the voice of God. He engaged his hearers. He knew what the message was and why it was important. He could apply it to the revelation unfolding in the presence of them all. He had perfectly integrated his being, his community, the synagogue, the role of the lector, and the proclamation of the reading. That is what lectors still aspire to do.

At Sunday Mass, Christians gather because we also honor the word of God. As we assemble to celebrate the Eucharist, we do not approach the table of communion until we have feasted at the table of the word.

> ✠ In the Mass the table both of God's word and of Christ's body is prepared, from which the faithful may be instructed and refreshed.
> — *General Instruction of the Roman Missal, #28*

"The Mass is made up, as it were, of two parts: the Liturgy of the Word and the Liturgy of the Eucharist. These, however, are so closely interconnected that they form but one single act of worship. For in the Mass the table both of God's word and of Christ's body is prepared, from which the faithful may be instructed and refreshed."[8]

In the scriptures, God speaks to us. At Mass, God speaks to a particular people gathered at a particular time in a particular place. The word will affect us in different ways. Each person will hear the message uniquely, as the Holy Spirit reaches into the hearts of us all to place within them the message that comes from God.

To work this miracle, God chooses instruments. God uses lectors.

A lector integrates many values. Lectors are people of faith who have nurtured a relationship with God and have formed their lives on the Gospel. They are members of a community of family, friends, and strangers, bound together by a desire to live near and for one another, and to share opportunities for faith and worship. Lectors have come to value their local Church and its mission. They understand the importance of making Sunday worship the highlight of their week. And they strive to make the reading of the scriptures a highlight of the Mass—because it is.

Lectors have personally encountered the word of God, and through them the people of God encounter the divine Word.

NOTES

1. Luke 4:18.

2. Ibid.

3. Ibid.

4. Ibid.

5. Luke 4:18–19.

6. Luke 4:21.

7. Hebrews 4:12.

8. *General Instruction of the Roman Missal*, #28. This is the principal document that describes and guides how Mass is celebrated. It was revised in 2001, with the English-language translation appearing in 2002. Hereafter, it is abbreviated as GIRM.

Welcome

You have agreed to serve the Church as a lector. A lector is any lay minister who reads from the Lectionary at Mass. In some locations a lector is called a reader. You will be entrusted with the word of God—a tool sharper than any two-edged sword. As any skilled craftsman does, you will want to know your tools in order to execute well your art.

About This Book

This book will help you. It will explain the significance of the role of lector and describe how to prepare for and fulfill your duties. It will answer some of the most frequently asked questions about the ministry. And it will invite you into a deeper experience of God through the Bible.

The Spirit of God came upon Jesus in a very special way. When he read that passage from Isaiah long ago, he absorbed its meaning as no other lector ever could or ever will. However, the Spirit of God is also upon you. God has placed the Spirit within you, a Holy Spirit who speaks to you, a Holy Spirit who uses you to proclaim the word of God.

About the Authors

This book was written by two authors. Paul Turner wrote the first sections of the book: the foreword, "Theology and History of the Ministry," and "Formation and Spirituality of the Lector." He is the pastor of St. Munchin parish in Cameron, Missouri, and its mission, St. Aloysius, in Maysville. A priest of the diocese of Kansas City–St. Joseph, he holds a doctorate in sacred theology from Sant' Anselmo in Rome. He is the author of many pastoral resources about sacraments and the liturgy.

Virginia Meagher wrote the practical description and explanation of the lector's duties in "Serving as Lector" and has provided the book's resource section and glossary. She has a BS in Communication Studies from Northwestern University, has done graduate studies in ministry at Loyola Universisty in Chicago, and has been involved in parish and archdiocesan liturgy for many years, including the Office for Divine Worship in the Archdiocese of Chicago. She is the Liturgical Coordinator for the diocese of Stockton in California.

Questions for Discussion and Reflection

1. Why have you agreed to serve as a lector?

_____

_____

_____

_____

_____

2. What do you hope to gain in your understanding of the theology and function of the ministry through this book?

_____

_____

_____

_____

_____

Theology and History of the Lector

God's Word in the Church and in Our Lives

The word of God calls us to follow. God speaks to us before we pray or respond. Our relationship does not begin with us speaking to God. It starts when God speaks.

The Old Testament recounts the story of a chosen people—not of a chosen God. God established a covenant with Abraham, Isaac, and Jacob. God renewed it with Moses and David. The holy men and women of old heard what God wanted and they responded in faith. God chose them. God spoke to them.

Jesus also illustrated this throughout his ministry. He preached in synagogues. He taught the crowds. Dramatically, he called disciples to come and follow him. Occasionally, a Gospel story makes it appear that someone else has made the first move. A rich young man asks if he can become a disciple. A woman approaches Jesus for a cure. But in every case, they have heard Jesus or heard about him. The Holy Spirit has opened their hearts, and they respond to the word of God.

When you first became a Christian through infant Baptism or the catechumenate, you took part in a liturgy about God's call. In the Rite of Acceptance into the Order of Catechumens, the community begins the Mass outside the church or by the door. The celebrant invites the new catechumens inside "to share with us at the table of God's word."[1] He then speaks to them briefly, helping them understand the dignity of God's word, which is proclaimed and heard in the church. From the first moment catechumens take their place in the assembly of the faithful, they learn that the Bible forms us.

Later on, before they are baptized, the celebrant may conduct a ceremony based on one of the cures from the Gospels. Jesus touched the ears and tongue of a man born unable to hear and speak clearly. In working the miracle, Jesus groaned out the Aramaic word *ephphatha*, which means "be opened."[2] Instantly, the man was healed. He became a

3

paradigm of discipleship. With his ears open and his tongue free, he could hear God's word and return full praise. When the celebrant touches the ears and lips of those being baptized, he speaks the same word Jesus did: *ephphatha*. To the evangelists, that unusual word was so powerful that they left it alone. They wrote the Gospels in Greek, but this word appears in its original language. We still use the same Aramaic word today. The celebrant says, "Ephphatha: that is, be opened, that you may profess the faith you hear, to the praise and glory of God."[3]

This ceremony may also be used in the Baptism of infants. As they are just beginning to learn the mysteries of human language, we pray that their ears will be opened to God's word, and that their lips will praise God all their days.[4]

These ceremonies show that our Christian lives begin with and thrive on the word of God. Engaging that word is the privilege and task of every Christian. God's word called us into discipleship. God's word guides us throughout discipleship. The more we open our ears, the more the scripture warms our heart and refreshes our perspective on life.

We hear God's word in many ways. We spend time with the Bible in private prayer. We refer to it when preparing for special events. We hear preachers and teachers cite specific passages. Most importantly, we hear the word of God proclaimed at Sunday Mass.

When we gather with other believers, we form the people of God. Together we have a task to perform: we offer praise to the one who sits on the throne and to the Lamb. While we are there, gathered as one in this sacred place, we open our ears together, so that God might speak to us. Most importantly, it is there at the Eucharist, in the presence of the community of believers, where we hear the word of God.

> ✠ [The faithful] form one body, whether by hearing the word of God, or by joining in the prayers and the singing, or above all by the common offering of Sacrifice and by a common partaking at the Lord's table.
>
> —*General Instruction of the Roman Missal, #96*

Listening is one of the ways that we express our unity. One of the duties of the people of God is to form one body, as paragraph 96 of the GIRM explains.

It is easier to seem one body when we perform the same action, assume the same posture, recite the same words or sing the same songs. But even when it looks like we are doing nothing—when we are listening—we are one. We are one when we unite our hearts in faith, when we hang onto every word as we do with those we love, when we make ourselves still, rather than miss a single word. When we do this together, we are one.

This is our joy. This is our duty: "All must listen with reverence to the readings from God's word, for they make up an element of greatest importance in the Liturgy."[5]

We all have a part to play when we come to Mass. We do not just attend Mass. We participate at Mass. When someone else is speaking, we participate. We listen. We open our ears and prepare our hearts to respond.

Oh yes, to respond. Jesus did not speak for his own entertainment. God did not invite Abraham and Sarah into the promises of the covenant just to fill the air with solemn sound. God's Word comes to us with a purpose. It demands a response.

"When God communicates his word, he expects a response, one, that is, of listening and adoring 'in Spirit and in truth' (John 4:23). The Holy Spirit

> *Be doers of the word and not hearers only.*
> —James 1:22

makes that response effective, so that what is heard in the celebration of the Liturgy may be carried out in a way of life: 'Be doers of the word and not hearers only' (James 1:22)."[6]

Our response, then, is twofold. When God speaks, we respond on the spot by listening and adoring. Then later we carry out the purpose of the scriptures in our way of life. All that we do is based upon the Word of God. It is our blueprint, our constitution, our mission statement, our compass.

Our response flows naturally when we realize what happens at Mass. God is speaking to us. This is not a mere reading of an ancient document, a report of something said long ago. It is not lines recited by an actor, not a mere recitation of a letter from someone you know.

God is speaking to us. When the scriptures are read, it is as if the book disappears. The lector becomes the mouthpiece of God. God uses the voice of the lector to say something modern, something new, something that applies to the world today. Yes, the words are old, but their proclamation is always new. To hear the scriptures proclaimed

> ✠ When the Sacred Scriptures are read in the Church, God himself speaks to his people, and Christ, present in his own word, proclaims the Gospel.
>
> —*General Instruction of the Roman Missal, #29*

is to hear the voice of God speaking right now to the people gathered together for worship.

The Gospel—more than the other readings—has a very special significance when it is proclaimed. The four Gospels contain the words that Jesus spoke. When a reading from them is proclaimed aloud in the context of the liturgy, Jesus is speaking his words—now, in your church, to you, and to the community. Jesus is speaking.

God has other ways to communicate with us, but this one is favored. God dwells apart from time. The sacred scriptures, written so long ago, still carry the voice of God today.

The lector has a daunting responsibility. The lector's voice needs to carry God's voice. The lector does not just pronounce words. The lector communicates a divine message.

The Liturgy of the Word within the Mass

The Mass takes place at two "tables"—the table of the word and the table of the Eucharist. But it is one table. The two parts of the Mass form one profound experience.

"In the Mass the table both of God's word and of Christ's Body is prepared, from which the faithful may be instructed and refreshed."[7]

The furniture is different. The Liturgy of the Word focuses on the ambo. The Liturgy of the Eucharist centers at the altar. These two furnishings draw the attention of the faithful throughout each part of the Mass.

There is one moment at the beginning, however, when the two parts of the Mass may be drawn together. In the entrance procession, the deacon—or in his absence a lector—may carry the Book of the Gospels to the sanctuary. Arriving there, the person carrying the book sets it on the altar, makes a reverence, and withdraws. This action does not take place with the Lectionary.

The Book of the Gospels, true to its name, is the collection of Gospel passages that may occur on Sundays or other major occasions throughout the year. It may be used for proclamation at any Mass. Having the Gospels in a separate book sets them apart from the other scriptures. The Gospels are special to us. When it is time to proclaim one at the Eucharist, the liturgy explodes with a variety of symbols. The people stand. The cantor begins the Gospel acclamation. If there is a deacon, he asks the priest for a blessing. If the priest reads the Gospel, he bows to the altar and prays humbly. A procession forms. Candles, incense, and other signs of honor may be carried. A special book is used. The deacon or priest greets the people. They respond. All trace the sign of the cross on their forehead, lips, and heart. The book may be incensed. And then, after all of that, after doing everything we can to draw attention to this book, we hear the words of Jesus.

The Book of the Gospels represents Christ. The altar, where the Liturgy of the Eucharist will be celebrated, also represents Christ. So at the beginning of Mass, these two symbols of Christ are brought together in a simple, yet meaningful gesture. The Book of the Gospels, carried up to the sanctuary in the entrance procession, is placed on the altar. The words of Jesus are set on the altar of Jesus. The Liturgy of the Word and the Liturgy of the Eucharist are joined as one.

The word of God deserves our respect. Lectors are not to change the texts for the introduction and conclusion of the reading, nor of the reading itself. The reading has been prepared by translators who worked hard on rendering the original language in a way it can be grasped when read aloud today. The translation has been approved by our bishops and confirmed by the Vatican for proclamation at the liturgy. The opening and closing formulas do not change because they serve the people. There is no need to introduce the opening formula with another formula, such as "The first reading is a reading from . . . ." Just announce, "A reading from. . . ." The people more easily open their ears to the reading when they hear the appropriate cue.

The word of God deserves our respect.

Indeed, the words take on a deep significance when they are repeated. The repetition of the words from church to church across the world, and from age to age throughout time, indicates their sanctity. The formulas have many layers of meaning that can be plumbed when they are used in the simplest of forms.

The reading closes when the lector says, "The word of the Lord." Some years ago, the lector used to conclude the reading with "This is the word of the Lord." But the conclusion was changed for various reasons. For example, the Latin text, on which the English translations of the parts of the Mass are based, has always had the lector say, "Verbum Domini," literally, "The word of the Lord."

The initial English translation made sense: "This is the word of the Lord." It made a simple declarative statement about the word that had been read. But in time, the meaning became obscured. Some lectors picked up the book before they announced, "This is the word of the Lord," as if the word were the book. It is not. The book is special, and it deserves to be handled with reverence because of its sacred contents and purpose. But the word is not the book. The word is the spoken word.

To many people, this seemed like a small point, but it aims to say something large: God still speaks to us. God's word is not past history. It is alive. The liturgy accentuates this reality in many ways.

The practice of distributing copies of the readings so that everyone can read along may seem helpful, but actually it confuses the meaning behind the proclamation of scripture. The word of God does not dwell in the communal *reading*, but in the communal *hearing*. When the lector is well prepared, when the people are listening and looking at the lector, when the book is less important than the voice, then the lector's words at the conclusion of the reading have an earthshaking meaning: "The word of the Lord." We have just heard God speak to us.[8]

The word of God does not dwell in the communal reading, but in the communal hearing.

The reading of sacred scripture has always been an important part of Christian worship. As we know from Jesus' own behavior, it was customary for readings to be proclaimed at the Jewish synagogue. Those early Christians who came from Judaism logically based their worship on ceremonial forms with which they were familiar. That included a reading.

Saint Paul asked those who received his letters to read them to other believers. At the end of the first letter to the Thessalonians, he commands the recipients to read the letter to the entire community.[9] The letter to the Colossians says, "And when this letter is read before you, have it read also in the church of the Laodiceans, and you yourselves read the one from Laodicea."[10] To the Corinthians, he writes, "For we write you nothing but what you can read and understand, and I hope that you will understand completely."[11]

The History of Lectors

The proclamation of scriptures at the Eucharist dates back at least as far as the time of Saint Justin. Writing about the year 150, he described a typical gathering of Christians. He wrote: "The memoirs of the apostles and the writings of the prophets are read, as much as time permits. . . . [The rest of the ceremony follows] when the reader has finished."[12] From this brief witness we recognize the customs of having regular readings and a lector to proclaim them.

It did not take long before some ceremony with the lector began to evolve. In some places in the third or fourth century, a ritual action was taking place before the reading began. The bishop picked up the book and handed it to the lector.[13] In this brief gesture the bishop indicated the worthiness of the book and his appointment of the reader to serve as a minister for the people.

The memoirs of the apostles and the writings of the prophets are read, as much as time permits.

—*Saint Justin, Apology 1:67*

From texts such as these it is clear that a Lectionary was used for Christian worship very early on, but no copies of such books have survived. The earliest one comes from the sixth century, and it was not as comprehensive as ours are today. Lectionaries continued to develop throughout the Middle Ages, and the one-year cycle of readings established after the Council of Trent served the Church for 400 years.

About the same time the ministry of reader changed from being a function of the laity to the responsibility of the ordained. Lay ministers proclaimed the scriptures from the earliest days of the Church, but eventually the title of lector became ceremonial and the task was absorbed into the duties of ordained ministers serving at the altar.

Before a man was ordained to the major order of priesthood, he passed through a series of rituals called minor orders. Originally, the minor orders appointed ministers to perform certain tasks, but in time they evolved into steps toward ordination to the priesthood. One of these made him a lector, but he was a lector more in name than in deed. There were some circumstances when a lector changed a reading, but normally this function was reserved to a minister of higher rank, the subdeacon.[14]

The Second Vatican Council made some changes to the ministry of lector. Pope Paul VI abolished the minor order of lector, a status attained when a bishop ordained a cleric to this function in a liturgical ceremony. But Pope Paul retained the title lector as an "instituted" lay ministry, a status still attained in a liturgical ceremony over which a bishop presides. Today's candidates for ordination are installed as "instituted" lectors before they can be ordained deacons or priests. But lectors are no longer considered clerics. The ministry has been returned to the laity who exercised it at the beginning of Church history. "By tradition, the function of proclaiming the readings is ministerial, not presidential."[15]

In theory, a person no longer has to be in preparation for priesthood to be "instituted" as a lector by a bishop. Pope Paul, however, kept the requirement that only lay *men* could be instituted as lectors. He permitted women and non-instituted men to read at Mass, but he did not allow women to be formally instituted in the ministry by a bishop.

Consequently, very few dioceses have a program of *instituted* lectors serving in parishes. Men and women share this ministry in parishes equally as *non-instituted, commissioned* lectors. They may obtain a certificate of service from the bishop, if that is the local custom, but they are not formally installed into the ministry by the bishop.

The *General Instruction of the Roman Missal* still makes some references to instituted lectors, as if they were common at Sunday Mass. For example, it expects instituted lectors to be vested (#336) and seated in the sanctuary (#195). But the GIRM does permit other commissioned laypersons to proclaim the readings at Mass: "In the absence of an instituted lector, other laypersons may be commissioned to proclaim the readings from Sacred Scripture. They should be truly suited to perform this function and should receive careful preparation."[16] The Church has been blessed by their service.

> ✛ In the absence of an instituted lector, other laypersons may be commissioned to proclaim the readings from Sacred Scripture.
>
> —*General Instruction of the Roman Missal, #101*

Our Lectionary

The Second Vatican Council also made changes to the Lectionary. The Sunday Lectionary expanded into a three-year cycle of readings denoting Years A, B, and C. During Ordinary Time, each year features one Gospel: Matthew, Mark, and Luke, respectively. The Gospel of John appears during the Easter season all three years, as well as on other occasions, such as the Second Sunday in Ordinary Time each year, many of the Sundays of Lent, and some of the summer Sundays of Year B.

On the Sundays of Ordinary Time, the first reading comes from somewhere in the Old Testament. It always bears a thematic relationship to the Gospel. During other times of the year, the first reading explores a theme relating to the season. For example, the first readings of Lent tell a sequence of stories from salvation history, leading up to the promise of our redemption. Over the course of three years, nearly all of the books of the Old Testament are represented in the Sunday Lectionary.

An exception to this plan occurs during the season of Easter. At that time, the first reading is drawn from the New Testament—from the Acts of the Apostles. There we hear the story of the apostolic Church, as it faced struggles and rejoiced in the promise of the Resurrection. For the seven weeks of Easter, all the readings come from the New Testament.

The responsorial psalm is chosen because it relates to a theme from the first reading. There are a few exceptions when the psalm pertains more to the season of the year or even to the Gospel. It is permissible to substitute another psalm that fits the occasion, especially if the parish has a musical setting of it in its repertoire.[17]

The second readings during Ordinary Time are semi-continuous excerpts of different New Testament books. For example, each year Ordinary Time begins with a series of readings from Paul's first letter to the Corinthians. Large parts of the letter are never read, but the passages we hear follow the thought of the letter from beginning to end over the entire three-year cycle. During the other times of the year, the second reading is chosen because it relates to the feast or season being celebrated. For example, the second readings of Advent show how the early Christians expected Christ would come again very soon, and how they challenged one another to live accordingly.

The Role of the Lector during Mass

The lector's role takes place during the Liturgy of the Word. The main parts of this first half of the Mass are the readings from sacred scripture and the music occurring between them. Periods of silence, the homily, the Creed, and the Prayer of the Faithful fill out the Liturgy of the Word.

Lectors should be trained:

Their preparation must above all be spiritual, but what may be called a technical preparation is also needed. The spiritual preparation presupposes at least a biblical and liturgical formation. The purpose of their biblical formation is to give readers the ability to understand the readings in context and to perceive by the light of faith the central point of the revealed message. The liturgical formation ought to equip the readers to have some grasp of the meaning and structure of the Liturgy of the Word and of the significance of its connection with the Liturgy of the Eucharist. The technical preparation should make the readers more skilled in the art of reading publicly, either with the power of their own voice or with the help of sound equipment.[18]

Lectors may serve on other occasions besides Mass, but they should be most familiar with their responsibilities at the Eucharist.

Lectors have the following duties. They join the entrance procession of the Mass, and they may carry the Book of the Gospels if there is no deacon present. Lectors proclaim the readings that precede the Gospel. They observe silences after each reading. If there is no one to sing the psalm, a lector may lead the refrain and proclaim the verses; however, it is preferable that the psalm be sung.[19]

If the deacon does not lead the Prayer of the Faithful, a lector may do so. If no one sings the entrance and communion antiphons of the Mass, and if the people do not recite them, the lector may read them.[20]

The lector's role concludes with the Liturgy of the Word. The lector continues, however, to participate fully at Mass throughout the Liturgy of the Eucharist. By custom, the lector does not walk out at the end of Mass in procession with the other ministers.[21] The lector leaves as a member of the faithful, all of whom are sent forth into the world to bring the word of God to all they meet.

The lector's services take up only a few minutes at Mass, but these are critical minutes. Even when processing to the altar at the beginning of Mass or to the ambo before the reading, the lector carries a sense of purpose. People will begin to comprehend the significance of the reading by the seriousness with which the lector approaches this task.

In the proclamation of the word, the people will realize how well the lector understands the reading. The lector's preparation will be evident by the way the reading sounds. The preparation is more than technical, grammatical, and mental. It is, above all, spiritual.

You have offered to serve your community as a lector. You have reflected on the gifts God gave you: a love for the Bible, an understanding of God's word, an ability to communicate, the willingness to proclaim the scripture in a public place, a love for the liturgy of the Church, and an appreciation of its calendar of feasts and seasons.

You will exercise a variety of functions: proclaiming the word, leading the psalm (if a cantor is not present), and offering the Prayer of the Faithful. You will need to grasp why these words are important each week—what it is that God is saying to the Church, and how the petitions express the hopes and desires of the local community.

> ✠ In the readings, as explained by the homily, God speaks to his people, opening up to them the mystery of redemption and salvation and offering them spiritual nourishment, and Christ himself is present in the midst of the faithful through his word.
>
> —*General Instruction of the Roman Missal, #55*

You will also be called upon to manage silences. Before you begin to read, you will want to have the attention of the entire assembly. After each reading you will pause and pray, modeling the reflection that all will do. Even the way you pace the petitions during the Prayer of the Faithful will help people think about them one by one. They will think about what circumstances need prayer this week and why these petitions have surfaced. Your recitation of these intentions will make it clear that you are anxious to pray them, inviting others to do so as well.

In order to "more fittingly and perfectly fulfill these functions," Paul VI recommends this profoundly direct expectation of a lector: you are "to meditate assiduously on the sacred Scripture."[22]

Questions for Reflection and Discussion

1. What was your experience with scripture when you were younger?

_____

_____

_____

_____

_____

2. Name a time when a passage from the Bible really moved you.

_____

_____

_____

_____

_____

3. Who are some lectors who have served as models for you? How did they read? How did they live?

_____

_____

_____

_____

_____

4. During the Liturgy of the Word at Mass, what do you do? What could you do?

_____

_____

_____

_____

_____

NOTES

1. *Rite of Christian Initiation of Adults*, #60.

2. Mark 7:34.

3. *Rite of Christian Initiation of Adults*, #199.

4. *Rite of Baptism for Children*, #65.

5. GIRM, #29.

6. *Lectionary for Mass*, #6.

7. *General Instruction of the Roman Missal*, #28.

8. Those who have a hearing impairment may benefit from a personal copy of the printed text or a live interpreter.

9. See 1 Thessalonians 5:27.

10. See Colossians 4:16.

11. See 2 Corinthians 1:13.

12. *Apology* 1:67. See *Catechism of the Catholic Church*, #1345.

13. *Apostolic Tradition*, #11.

14. After receiving the minor orders, a candidate was ordained to the major orders of subdeacon, deacon, and priest. These ministers vested for Mass and performed assigned functions. The subdiaconate was eliminated after the Second Vatican Council.

15. GIRM, #59.

16. GIRM, #101.

17. GIRM, #61.

18. Introduction to the *Lectionary for Mass,* #55.

19. GIRM, #61.

20. GIRM, #194–198.

21. See page 61, note 3, in this resource. If the lector has been instituted, is vested in the garb proper to the ministerial role, and has been sitting in the sanctuary for Mass, he would walk out with other ministers at the end. However, the Book of the Gospels is not processed out at the end of Mass. Be familiar with the customs of your parish and diocese.

22. Apostlic Letter issued *Motu Proprio,* by which the Discipline of First Tonsure, Minor Orders, and Subdiaconate in the Latin Church is Reformed, in *The Installation of Readers and Acolytes, Admission to Candidacy for Ordination as Deacons and Priests.* International Committee on English in the Liturgy, Inc. 1976.

Spirituality and Formation of the Lector

The Spirit of the Lord is upon me.

—*Luke 4:18*

The lector is the mouthpiece through which God speaks to the Church. Lectors are effective when they open their ears to hear God's word and open their hearts to love God's people.

Lectors take care of their spirit. Just as athletes care for their bodies, as teachers train their minds, as musicians practice to refine their art, as firefighters rehearse procedures for safety, so lectors spend time with the Spirit. Being a lector is not just having a ministry—it is being a certain kind of person.

Nurturing your spirit gives God more ways to use you. You will be God's servant in ways beyond imagining.

The Spirituality of Sunday Mass

The most important activity of your life is your regular participation at Sunday Mass. You do not have to be a lector to know this is true.

Sunday is the Lord's Day, the day when we commemorate the rising of Christ from the dead. Our celebration of the Eucharist expresses our belief in the Resurrection of Christ, and our hope that one day we shall share glory with him in the Father. To participate in Mass is to take a stand for our belief in God, who created our life, who sent Jesus into the world, and who promised the Holy Spirit, the giver of charity. Sunday belongs to the Lord; we devote our time to God.

Sunday is also a day of leisure. It should feel different from other days. People often say it should not be hard to set aside one hour a week for God. That is true, but a fruitful celebration of Mass will require more time. It will take time for leisure, especially before Mass. It will be hard to participate if we are busy up to the time we leave home to go to church. Our minds and bodies need time to prepare. You don't exercise without first stretching. You don't have heat in the car until it warms up. The time before Mass is spent preparing our minds and hearts for what we soon will do. We will place ourselves in God's presence, concentrate on the words and gestures of the service, and form a community of believers.

While you are at church, even if you are not serving as lector that day, put your heart, will, mind, and strength into the Eucharist. As a member of the assembly, you will be called upon to sing songs, make responses, assume postures, make gestures, and observe silences. As a lector, you are a leader, a model for the behavior of others. People will do what you do. If you model participation and prayer for them even when you are not in the ambo, they will more gratefully follow your words when you are.

You are responsible for helping to form the community at Sunday Mass. While you speak, all will listen as one body. You can also help to form this community by getting to know the other people at church. Spend some time before and after Mass visiting with people and getting to know how they are. If you are not good at names, practice them. Obtain a parish directory. After Mass make a note about the people you met today, so you can seek them out the next time.

You are responsible for helping to form the community at Sunday Mass.

It takes time to learn the names of people in a parish, but it is worth the effort. You will feel more and more at home at church, and people will feel more and more at home with you as their reader.

Especially if part of your ministry is to lead the petitions for the Prayer of the Faithful, you will want to know how to pray for the people you lead. You will come to learn their joys and sorrows. You bring all these with you into the ambo. There, as you read, you proclaim a word that challenges and comforts, that makes people question and offers them hope. There, as you pray, you sense more urgently the concerns the community needs to lift to God.

Sunday Mass is the most important activity of your week. There you give your heart to God and lend an ear to your neighbor. There you praise God for the gift of life and Resurrection, and you work at forming the community of believers who put their trust in God.

Cultivating Spirituality through the Lectionary

The Bible makes a good companion for every Christian's prayer. The Lectionary is an especially good prayer resource for the lector.

Years ago, Catholics were actually discouraged from reading the Bible. Authorities were afraid that people would misinterpret what it says. Catholics used their Bibles as record books—places where the names of children, the choice of spouses, and the dates of death were recorded. They rested on coffee tables or nearby shelves. But rarely did Catholics use Bibles for prayer.

It is fitting to commend the names of the family to pages of the Bible. But it is more fitting to read the word of God.

Today, the Catholic Church includes a wider variety of scripture readings in a typical Sunday Mass than in the past. Readings from scripture form an integral part of our worship outside of Mass as well. As a Church we have recommitted ourselves to the word of God, and many individuals have discovered its beauty as well.

As a Church we have recommitted ourselves to the word of God.

For lectors, a Lectionary offers an ideal way to use the Bible for prayer and study. (Paperback study editions can be purchased; see page 63 in the resource section.) The Lectionary is the collection of readings used for Mass and other principal celebrations of the Church. It does not include every line of the Bible. It does include those parts of the Bible deemed most useful for Christians to know, arranged in a helpful way. It doesn't look like an abridged Bible, but in a way, it is.

Lectors can find out which readings are appointed for any given Sunday by consulting any number of different tools, but it would be good for lectors to learn how the Lectionary is organized.

If you do not own your own, take a look at the one in church sometime. The Lectionary requires four volumes. The first is the one you use the most. It contains the readings for Sunday. The second and third volumes are used for weekdays, and the fourth has collected the readings for other special occasions.

Sundays

The first volume, though, is the one you should know the best. Notice that the book is arranged by seasons: Advent, Christmas, Lent, Easter, and Ordinary Time. There is a section for solemnities of the Lord during Ordinary Time, where you find the readings for days like the

If the number of the calendar year is divisible exactly by three, we are in Year C.

Most Holy Trinity and the Most Holy Body and Blood of Christ. Many lectors find these readings difficult to locate.

Each Sunday offers readings for Years A, B, and C. If the number of the calendar year is divisible exactly by three, then we are in Year C. You can figure out Year A and B from there. The liturgical year begins, of course, with the Advent that precedes the new calendar year.

Weekdays

On weekdays during Ordinary Time the first reading is on a two-year cycle, but the Gospel remains the same each year. At the beginning of Ordinary time the Lectionary presents a semi-continuous reading of Mark, considered to be the oldest of the four Gospels. It then moves to Matthew and concludes with Luke. During the seasons of the year (Advent, Christmas, Lent, and Easter), we hear the same first reading each year and the same Gospel reading. Excerpts from the Gospel of John are proclaimed during these seasons especially during the second half of Lent and throughout the Easter season. To simplify things for the lector, the readings of each year are kept in separate ritual books. We use Year I readings in odd-numbered years and Year II readings in even-numbered years. Years I and II begin with the Advent that precedes the odd- and even-numbered calendar years, respectively.

Special Occasions

Volume four contains the readings for special occasions: Marriages, funerals, Baptisms, and a host of other events. If you are ever looking for a particular passage from the Bible to fit a certain circumstance, it is worth looking at volume four. You may not find the exact theme you need, but once you become familiar with the contents of the book, it will be easier to locate useful passages.

Navigating through the Lectionary

In the front of the Lectionary you will find several tables.[1] One of them shows you which Lectionary cycle falls during which year. It also gives the date for some moveable feasts such as Ash Wednesday, Easter, and Pentecost. It will tell you how many weeks of Ordinary Time will fall between the Christmas season and Lent. It will also say which week of Ordinary Time will resume on what day when the Easter season is over.

Another table gives the order of the second readings in Ordinary Time. If you're interested, you can see at a glance which books of the Bible you will be reading during Ordinary Time this year.

In the second appendix of the Lectionary is a complete chart of scripture readings found in the Lectionary. It is arranged according to the books of the Bible, starting with Genesis and ending with Revelation. If you know a citation and you wonder where to find it in the four-volume Lectionary, you can look it up in the second appendix.

One of the more important skills a lector can develop is how to figure out why a particular reading is chosen for any given day. You can find some help for this in the Lectionary, but you often have to use your imagination. You will find a most helpful introduction to the Lectionary in the front of the first volume. Chapter four is called "The General Arrangement of Readings for Mass," and chapter five is the "Description of the Order of Readings." Paragraphs 64 through 68 explain the principles behind the choice of texts for Sundays. Paragraphs 92 through 110 explain the rationale behind the choice of readings season by season.

Lectors familiar with these principles will understand another layer beneath the scripture they read. They certainly want to come to know the meaning of the passage as it appears in the Bible—what book it is from, what part of the *You will find a most helpful introduction to the Lectionary in the front of the first volume.* narrative it tells, what problems it is answering, or what part of an extended argument it makes. But they will also want to know the meaning of this passage as it appears in the Lectionary. Why was it chosen for this particular day? Does it have a theme that relates to the Gospel? Is there a word or phrase that sounds the theme of the season of the year we are in? Is it simply a continuation of a passage we heard last Sunday? Answers to these questions are critical if the lector is to nuance the reading in a way that lends coherence to the entire Liturgy of the Word.

For this reason, it will help you to have some familiarity with all the scriptures of any given Sunday, even those you do not proclaim, including the psalm. The psalm is often chosen as a direct response to the first reading. If you will be reading the first reading, consider why the psalm for that day fits. What will the Gospel be, and how does it fulfill the ideas germinating in your text? If you see how all the readings of a given day interrelate, you will read with greater understanding.

By spending time studying the Lectionary, you are deepening your appreciation of the spiritual task you do. Your love for the word of God will grow as you become more familiar with the way our Church proclaims it and hears it.

Prayer at Home

Everyone is encouraged to pray at home. The early Christians made it a habit twice a day—morning and evening. If it was getting light or getting dark, it was getting to be time to pray.

Do you set aside some time at home for prayer? What resources do you use? Do you incorporate passages from the Bible? Are the Sunday scriptures part of your weekly prayer?

Many lectors like to make the Lectionary part of their prayer at home. If you know the citations for the weekday readings, for example, you could read one or more of them as part of your meal prayer. Or, in anticipation of the weekend, you could read the coming Sunday scriptures throughout the week. You could read one a day, including the psalm. Or you could read more than one a day and repeat them at other meals. The more you hear the word of God, the more it can penetrate your very being.

One method of praying the scriptures has traditionally been called *lectio divina*. It is a process of slow meditation on the word of God. When you read the morning paper or an assignment for class or a light novel, you probably do it as quickly as you can. But *lectio divina* is a slow reading of the word of God. Try the following. Calm yourself and prepare your heart to acquire an attitude of prayer. Read slowly the passage you are going to proclaim on Sunday. Did something in the text grab your attention? Reflect a while on that word or phrase. Memorize it. Pray about it: tell God what is on your mind about those words. Then rest in the presence of God, who comes to you in this word. Read the passage slowly again, and let it speak to you more deeply than it did the first time.

Take some time with these scriptures. Some people like to journal. Find a quiet place and time at home. Read over the scriptures for this coming week. Jot down a few thoughts about them. Return to the same readings later on. Write some more. How is God speaking to you personally through these readings? Before you present these readings to the entire community, have you wrestled with them yourself? Before you shoulder the job of saying God's word to others, have you asked yourself, "What is God saying to me?"

Before you present these readings to the entire community, have you wrestled with them yourself?

Some people like a more structured prayer, such as the Liturgy of the Hours. Morning and Evening Prayer are especially beautiful. They give you a generous helping of psalms and canticles for your reflection, as well as a short scripture passage during each prayer. But don't let the brevity of this passage mislead you. It contains only a few words, so that you can hear them, meditate on them, and act on them. There are many ways to pray with the word of God.

Spiritual Reading about Scripture

Many people who have studied the Bible in depth have authored commentaries on the various books of scripture. Such a book can help you understand more of the passages you read and feed you great insights. There are good overviews of the entire Bible, as well as journals dedicated to biblical studies. These are written on a variety of levels. Some require very little previous understanding of the Bible. Others are for more devoted scholars.

Treat yourself to a good book about the Bible or a commentary on a part of the Bible that appeals to you. Read it in small doses and let it nourish your appreciation of God's word.

Treat yourself to a good book about the Bible.

Retreat Days

Look for opportunities to learn more about the Bible. There may be a retreat center near where you live. Take advantage of the days they offer for prayer and meditation. Attend a retreat of several days once a year if you are able. Take a spiritual book or a biblical commentary with you to a special place where you can spend some time reading slowly with understanding.

Pay attention to how other people use scripture. How did the homilist preach about the readings this week? Did the message surprise you? If you heard a spiritual talk this week, how did the speaker quote scripture? Which passages were used? Why? Which words of the Bible are quoted in articles you read or songs you sing?

Spiritual Conversation

When you have spiritual conversation with others, rely on the scriptures for help. When someone shares his or her joys or sorrows with you, think for a few moments about the Bible. Is there something in the life of Jesus that reminds you of what this person is going through? Is there some story from the Old Testament or a passage from the epistles that sheds light on this situation? Is there a psalm that captures the spirit of what this person is going through?

Challenge yourself to name a passage from the Bible that applies to different situations in life. It will increase your familiarity with the Bible and your ability to relate it to the various emotional phases we undergo.

Prayers

Prayers you may find helpful are offered here and at the beginning and end of the book.

If a priest is to read the Gospel at Mass, he says this before he begins: "Almighty God, cleanse my heart and my lips that I may worthily proclaim your Gospel."

After the reading, the deacon or the priest says, "May the words of the Gospel wipe away our sins."

Several of the psalms sing praise to God's word. Psalm 19 is one that may be sung at the Easter Vigil. The refrain for this particular responsory comes from a story in the Gospel of John. Some disciples were turning away from Jesus because they could not accept his teaching on the Eucharist. Jesus was afraid even the Twelve would go. But Peter spoke on behalf of the others: "Lord, you have the words of everlasting life."[2]

This lovely sentiment is paired with a psalm honoring the law of God, the sacred Torah, the holy word in which we find all wisdom. The psalm is filled with synonyms for God's word: law, decree, precepts, command, and ordinances. They are sweeter than honey.

Responsorial Psalm   *Psalm 19:8, 9, 10, 11*

R: Lord, you have the words of everlasting life.

The law of the LORD is perfect,
    refreshing the soul;
the decree of the LORD is trustworthy,
    giving wisdom to the simple.

R: Lord, you have the words of everlasting life.

The precepts of the LORD are right,
    rejoicing the heart;
the command of the LORD is clear,
    enlightening the eye.

R: Lord, you have the words of everlasting life.

The fear of the LORD is pure,
    enduring forever;
the ordinances of the LORD are true,
    all of them just.

R: Lord, you have the words of everlasting life.

They are more precious than gold,
*   than a heap of purest gold;*
sweeter also than syrup
*   or honey from the comb.*

R: Lord, you have the words of everlasting life.

Cultivating Spirituality through Service

Every Christian is called to serve others, and the lector should be especially prepared to do so. Your service at the ambo is not about you. It is about the word of God. Throughout your life, you strive to decrease, so that Christ may increase in you. When people hear you read, they will hear God speak. And when people see you act, they should see Christ act.

You probably already offer service to others in a variety of ways—to your family, your neighbors, people at church, at work, and even to complete strangers. But you might give some thought to types of service that especially fit your ministry as a reader.

Give some thought to types of service that especially fit your ministry as a reader. When do you read the Bible to others? Would residents at a nursing home like you to read passages for them? Would the catechumens in your parish like to know how you prepare to read and what the word of God means to you? Do you encourage other people to turn to the Bible? Buy several extra Bibles so you can give one away when you learn in conversation that someone doesn't own one. Would the chaplain's office at a local hospital or prison like to have a donation of Bibles or a volunteer who would read scripture there?

Are there children who need special help? In local schools, are there pupils struggling to learn how to read? Would their teachers welcome a volunteer assistant? Do you have neighbors who have English as a second language? Are you patient with them, helping them to read and to speak?

Give some thought to the service of the word. When you stand at the ambo, you want to be a person so completely imbued with the word of God, that it forms who you are, how you live, and how you serve other people.

Silence

The signature task of any lector is reading. But every lector must also be comfortable with silence. The GIRM (#56) says, "The Liturgy of the Word is to be celebrated in such a way as to promote meditation, and so any sort of haste that hinders recollection must clearly be avoided."

We live in a busy culture. We rarely stop to think. We fill our empty spaces with noise and colors. We avoid the silence, because silence makes us think, and thinking gives us insight, and insight may challenge us to live a different way, to rethink our values, to pick up a cross, and to follow Christ.

If you aspire to be a good lector, be good at silence. Make time each day to quiet your heart. Prepare yourself before you read. Use pauses while you read. The Word of God is truly present in the proclaimed word. And the Spirit of God is truly present in the silences.

If you aspire to be a good lector, be good at silence.

You have entered a holy place. You go up to the ambo to read. You center yourself. You experience God in your heart and in the community gathered before you. You open the Lectionary. You see the words of Isaiah. All eyes are fixed on you. You take a breath. Rather, you take in the Breath. And you say, "The Spirit of the Lord is upon me."[3]

Questions for Reflection and Discussion

1. How do you use the Bible for prayer at home?

_____

_____

_____

_____

_____

2. This week, how have you heard someone use a passage from the Bible? What did it say to you?

_____

_____

_____

_____

3. Apart from the liturgy, how do you use the written word or the spoken word in service to others in your community?

_____

_____

_____

_____

4. When is the quietest part of your day? When is the noisiest?

_____

_____

_____

_____

NOTES

1. These tables appear in the *front* of the ritual edition of the Lectionary, but at the *back* of the study edition.

2. See John 6:68c. See also Psalm 19 from the Easter Vigil (Lectionary #41ABC).

3. See Luke 4:18.

Serving as a Lector

Ezra read plainly from the book of the law of God, interpreting it so that all could understand what was read. Then Nehemiah, that is, His Excellency, and Ezra the priest-scribe and the Levites who were instructing the people said to all the people: "Today is holy to the LORD your God. Do not be sad, and do not weep"—for all the people were weeping as they heard the words of the law.

—*Nehemiah 8:8–10*

Overview of the Role of the Lector

When was the last time the beauty and the joy of hearing the word of God proclaimed in our assemblies made the people weep?

"[Lectors] should receive careful preparation, so that the faithful by listening to the readings from the sacred texts may develop in their hearts a warm and living love for Sacred Scripture."[1] Do you personally feel that the prepared and practiced reading of scripture at Mass has led you to a warm and living love for scripture?

Now that you are preparing to be a lector, it falls to you to bring this power of the word of God and love of scripture to others. If this sounds daunting, remember that you have been brought to ministry in the midst of a community that loves and respects you enough to trust you to be the voice of God in their midst. Some nervousness may always be natural, and a healthy sense of humility in the face of what you are doing is exceedingly appropriate. But remember also that you are already skilled and blessed and that the community believes you are well suited for this ministry. Through resources such as this book and training sessions at your parish, you are receiving the careful preparation that will allow you to lead others to the love of scripture that you already possess.

The Lectionary and the Seasons

The Lectionary is the best place to start your preparation—both in the ministry of lector and as the particular lector for any celebration. A careful and prayerful reading of the scriptures during the week leading up to Sunday will open you to the many ways in which the Liturgy of the Word is intimately connected to the entire liturgical celebration.

It is also particularly helpful to read through the cycle of readings for an entire season, especially Advent, Christmas, Lent, and Easter. This broad overview will put your ministry not only in the context of a particular Sunday, but also in the entire seasonal movement in which we are engaged as a people. Each Mass leads us through the mystery of Christ's Passion, death, and Resurrection. Each season does the same in an even broader context, focusing us on preparing for God's living presence in our lives here and now, celebrating the fullness of joy at the word of God alive in our midst, calling us back to our Lord when we have fallen away, and leading us to marvel at the tomb still empty and resplendent in the glory of Resurrection and never ending life. The season of Ordinary Time also leads us to a greater and deeper appreciation of the mystery of God in our own lives and in the lives of our communities and the world (see the chart on page 31.

It is particularly helpful to read through the cycle of readings for an entire season.

This repetition of seasons and readings over the years should not lead us to be complacent in our preparation. Each time we approach our ministry we do so with openness to where God is and where God is calling us now. At some point, we have probably each heard a deacon or priest begin the reading with the words "In those days a decree went out from Caesar Augustus that the whole world should be enrolled,"[2] and by the word "Augustus" we knew the rest of the reading and were looking at the poinsettias in the sanctuary, gazing at the stained-glass windows, and thinking about our crèche scene at home. We may have heard a reading year after year, one that we know so well that we have it labeled in our minds ("The Three Magi," "The Prodigal Son"). But our challenge as lectors in our preparation and in our participation at each Mass is to be truly open to hearing the entire reading and its call to us here and now.

Liturgical Season	Primary Theme or Focus*
Advent	First Two Weeks: • The second coming of Christ reigning over all creation in glory • Longing and waiting for the return of the Lord Second Two Weeks: • Preparing to celebrate the Incarnation • Recalling the birth of Christ
Christmas	Celebration of the Incarnation: • Wedding of heaven and earth • Manifestation of God in Jesus Christ in the Incarnation • Light in the darkness • Coming of the reign of God
Ordinary Time, Winter	• The beginning of Christ's public life and ministry • Living out the Paschal Mystery
Lent	*Preparation for the renewal of our Baptism:* • A recommitment to our faith • A deepening of our conversion to Christ and the Gospel *Journeying with the elect as they prepare for their Baptism:*
Triduum	*Commemoration of the Passion, death, and Resurrection of Christ:*
Easter	• The risen Christ among us • New and eternal life
Ordinary Time, Summer and Autumn	• Living out the Paschal Mystery • The approach of the end times

*This table was composed by D. Todd Williamson.

One of the great joys of our faith is that we can never delve too deeply into mystery. While we may know these readings well, we can hear them differently each time we encounter them. As the years go by, we change and grow and are not quite the same as we were when last this scripture was proclaimed to us. We can assume the same of the entire assembly gathered: that over time we all change. We face births and deaths in our families, joys and setbacks in our lives, and we continue to encounter God speaking to us through his word. If we truly listen in our preparation and at Mass, we may hear what we have not heard in a reading before or be called back to something we have heard but need to hear again. We can never allow the repetition of the seasons or the cycle of readings to keep us from recognizing that this time of listening is a fresh and new encounter with our Lord.

The presence of God in the word makes it critical that we as lectors are prepared and that we do not improvise or add any personal touch to our ministry. Lectors must help the assembly to focus on the word of God, and not on any of us personally. Whether we are discussing movement, proclamation, or our presence as a minister, we do everything with humility so that the focus is properly kept on the word of God and not on us.

The Lector's Role during Mass

The lector's tasks may vary from parish to parish. They depend on whether there is a deacon, how many lectors are assigned to a Mass, and so forth. What follows is a general overview. It is important that you know about any variations at your parish before you begin your ministry.

Our first responsibility as a lector is to arrive early (15 to 20 minutes before the start of Mass, depending on your parish) and to sign in. This is important because it ensures that people are in place ahead of time and there is no last minute wondering *if* you are going to arrive. This is also important for you in your ministry because it allows you to check in, greet the other ministers, go to the ambo and ensure that you know exactly where in the Lectionary your reading is, adjust the microphone, pray silently before Mass, and prepare yourself mentally to serve the community well. Depending on your personal temperament, you may need even a little more time to prepare yourself than your church requires. Feel

Arrive early!

free to come even earlier if that is helpful. Coming later than asked, however, makes both you and the other ministers rushed, anxious, and unfocused for the liturgy. Do your utmost to avoid this.

At many parishes, the lectors will be a part of the opening procession. If this is not the case in your parish, you should be in your seat five minutes before Mass so that you are ready to go. If you will be a part of the opening procession however, you should be gathered with the other ministers and ready for that role whenever you are asked to be there, or at least five minutes before Mass begins.

The opening procession will be led by the altar server with the incense if it is used, then the cross bearer and candle bearers, and then the lectors. If there is no deacon and your parish has a Book of the Gospels, then you may be asked to carry it in procession. If so, you will follow the other lector and hold the book slightly elevated (not with arms straight above your head, but in front of you and slightly higher than your face; see the photo on page vi). When the procession reaches the sanctuary, you make a profound bow to the altar and then proceed to your seat. If you are carrying the Book of the Gospels, however, omit the bow, place the Book of the Gospels reverently on the altar, and proceed to your seat.[3]

After the Opening Prayer is concluded, the assembly will sit down. At this point the priest celebrant may offer a few words of introduction to the readings. If there is a children's Liturgy of the Word, the children will be dismissed at this point. It is important to know if there will be something happening after the opening prayer and before the first reading. Once the assembly is seated, the first lector proceeds to the ambo. The Lectionary has already been placed there, open to the first reading. Take a moment before beginning to ensure that people are settled and able to listen.

The ritual language that begins the reading is very important: "A reading from the . . . ." It is not appropriate to begin in any other way or with any other words. The Lectionary will have the introductory words at the top of the reading. In a clear and firm voice, proclaim exactly what the Lectionary specifies. Then pause for a moment. If at all possible, *Proclaim exactly what the Lectionary specifies.* this should be done while looking at the people, and not at the Lectionary. Because of your preparation before the Mass you will know exactly what book the reading is from.

After the reading is proclaimed it is appropriate to pause for a moment, look up, and address the assembly with the words: "The word of the Lord." Wait for the assembly's response. Pause for a few moments of silence, and then proceed back to your seat.

The psalmist should allow a bit of silence after the lector sits down, so that people can remember and reflect on the word they have just heard. The length of that silence will depend on the parish, although a good rule of thumb is to wait at least the length of a mentally recited Hail Mary. This should be a prayerful and meditative recitation—not rushed. An exact length is not specified, but it is important for all ministers to be comfortable with silence. The more we as lectors are comfortable with silence, the more the assembly will also be comfortable with silence.

> ✠ Any sort of haste that hinders recollection must clearly be avoided.
>
> —*General Instruction of the Roman Missal, #56*

> The Liturgy of the Word is to be celebrated in such a way as to promote meditation, and so any sort of haste that hinders recollection must clearly be avoided. During the Liturgy of the Word, it is also appropriate to include brief periods of silence, accommodated to the gathered assembly, in which, at the prompting of the Holy Spirit, the word of God may be grasped by the heart and a response through prayer may be prepared. It may be appropriate to observe such periods of silence, for example, before the Liturgy of the Word itself begins, after the first and second reading, and lastly at the conclusion of the homily.[4]

The psalmist will then proceed to the ambo for the proclamation of the psalm. While this is a scripture reading, ritual language (such as "A reading from Psalm . . .") does not precede it. Instead, the psalmist begins with the response and then, with a gesture, invites the assembly to repeat the response. At the end of the psalm, the psalmist returns to his or her place. Please note that "it is preferable that the Responsorial Psalm be sung."[5] "The Christian faithful who gather together as one to await the Lord's coming are instructed by the Apostle Paul to sing together psalms, hymns, and spiritual songs (cf. Colossians 3:16)."[6] If a cantor is not available, then a lector may recite the psalm.

Once the psalmist has stopped moving, the lector proclaiming the second reading will rise and go to the ambo. The same instructions apply for the second reading as for the first. After the assembly has responded to that reading with "Thanks be to God," pause for a few moments, and then be seated. (If the community has a Book of the Gospels, the lector may need to move the Lectionary to a lower shelf of the ambo or to a nearby table or seat, depending on the arrangements of the parish.)

Again, it is appropriate to observe a few moments of silence following the second reading. As the Gospel acclamation begins, the assembly stands. If there is a Gospel procession, it may include incense, candles, and the Book of the Gospels. Once at the ambo, the Gospel reader (the deacon or, if no deacon is present, a priest) proceeds in the same manner as the first and second lectors. At the conclusion of the Gospel, the Book of the Gospels is left on the ambo. The homily follows.

After the homily there is a third period of silence so that the people have a chance to reflect prayerfully on what they have heard. Then the assembly stands to profess our faith. As the Profession of Faith ends, if you are reading the Prayer of the Faithful, you will move up to the ambo "or another suitable place"[7] for the proclamation. If there is a deacon at the Mass, he should read the prayers from the ambo or "another suitable place."[8] They are read clearly and everyone responds with the spoken or sung response. Only after the priest celebrant has read the concluding prayer for the Prayer of the Faithful, do you leave the ambo and return to your seat.

As the Liturgy of the Eucharist begins, the role of the lector is finished in most parishes. The Book of the Gospels is not processed out of the church at the end of Mass.

Other Responsibilities of a Lector

Aside from arriving early, checking in, getting ready, and proclaiming well, you have several other responsibilities as a lector.

The priest, liturgical ministers, and indeed the entire assembly depend on you to be present for your ministry. Lectors are generally scheduled in advance for specific readings at specific Masses on specific days. You are responsible for ensuring you know when you are scheduled, and that you are prepared for and present for those Masses.

If you cannot participate in a particular Mass for which you are scheduled, it is your responsibility to find a substitute from among the other lectors at your parish. If this is not possible, inform the coordinator of lectors as soon as possible so that other arrangements can be made.

You may be asked to read the Prayer of the Faithful; this is also a significant part of your ministry. "In the Prayer of the Faithful, the people respond in a certain way to the word of God which they have welcomed in faith and, exercising the office of their baptismal priesthood, offer prayers to God for the salvation of all."[9] It is important that you practice these prayers in advance so that they do not sound like announcements, but the true expression of the people's petitions. There is often a petition for those who are sick or those who have died that will include one or more names. The community prays for these people because they are a part of the body of Christ and their presence or absence affects us all. It is important that their names are pronounced correctly and are recognizable to the assembly, so be sure to ask someone in authority if you are unsure how to pronounce a name. It is a great privilege to proclaim the prayer of the entire community, and your preparation should reflect this.

Practice these prayers in advance so that they do not sound like announcements, but the true expression of the people's petitions.

Finally, even after you have been a lector for some time and feel that you are fairly skilled at the ministry, you are responsible for ensuring that you receive ongoing formation. This can take many forms, including advanced public speaking courses and additional scripture studies. However you choose to continue to grow in this ministry, it is important to remember that the assembly is always counting on you to continue to bring life and meaning to the text you are proclaiming.

Overall, it is a very straightforward ministry, and the better you are prepared for it, the simpler and more transparent it will appear to those gathered in worship. But there is real work that needs to go into making the practiced and carefully considered appear simple and truly transparent. As Saint Benedict wrote in his Rule, "the reader should not be the one who just happens to pick up the book, but someone who will read for a whole week, beginning on Sunday . . . . Brothers will read and sing, not according to rank, but according to their ability to benefit their hearers."[10]

Next we will look at the skills, preparation, practice, and reflection that will help you proclaim the scriptures so as to inspire in the hearts of the assembly a love for the word of God.

Skills for Proclaiming the Word of God

The willingness of your parish to train you as a lector indicates that you already possess at least a good basic skill set on which to build, but you will learn many others to enhance your work as a lector. Good public speaking skills will help you in this ministry, and so will good reading skills and the ability to pray with the Bible. There is always more to learn about understanding and proclaiming the scriptures, so we should never let a feeling of accomplishment stop us from diligently trying to do better. A spirit of humility, awe for the word of God, and a deep sense of responsibility to the community will help us approach this ministry well.

Developing a Method for Preparation

Among the many ways that you can prepare each week for your ministry, it is often helpful to gather with other lectors from the parish. Meeting early in the week to discuss the genres and themes, pray through the scriptures, and practice your proclamation can give insight and support for the work. When it is not possible to reflect on the scripture with others, the work of preparation can be done individually.

Preparation is particularly important, because through it we can reflect deeply on both the word of God and on the means of proclaiming that word. Scripture is not simply another piece of literature. Detailed study and reflection on the reading allow us to move past the mechanics of being a lector and be truly disposed to enter into the mystery of God's word. When we ourselves are awakened to the mystery of scripture and its proclamation, then we can bring that mystery to the assembly and truly serve our communities well. If we just worry about the mechanics of the reading, we will provide a good public speaking performance, but it may be difficult to bring to the people the sense of awe and wonder that the ministry requires.

> *When we ourselves are awakened to the mystery of scripture, then we can bring that mystery to the assembly.*

Identifying Genre, Speaker, Theme, and Voice

Understanding the genre, speaker, and theme of the reading will go a long way toward determining the most effective way to proclaim it. Genres are literary types that have a characteristic style, form, and subject matter. There are several *genres* that occur frequently in the Lectionary.

NARRATIVE: A narrative is a story. We often encounter these in the first readings from the Old Testament and the Acts of the Apostles. Think of the stories of the people of Israel crossing the Red Sea, wandering in the desert, and crying out for lack of water. Remember the stories of the first Christian community that we hear during the Easter season. The narrator of the story is usually an unidentified storyteller with no role in the action.

DISCOURSE: A discourse is generally a speech, lecture, or letter that makes an argument or explanation. Discourse can be found in the Gospel readings in the sermons of Jesus. The Sermon on the Mount or the Sermon on the Plain or the five "Bread of Life" readings from the Gospel of John (in the midst of Ordinary Time during the summer in Year B) are good examples of discourses. The writings of Paul or the other epistle writers are often discourses. They are addressed to specific communities in order to clarify theology, make arguments for the Christian life, and exhort the audience to live it more fully. They probably respond to questions the writer has received. Readings that are discourses usually have clearly identifiable speakers.

POETRY: Poems can be recognized most often by their layout on the page, but also by their metaphors, repetition, and cadence, as they speak to the deeper truths of God and life. The beautiful creation story from Genesis 1, although presented in paragraph layout, is unmistakably poetic. Poetry can be seen in the sometimes thundering, sometimes comforting proclamations of the prophets, the laments of Job, the versified advice of the wisdom books, and the awe-inspiring visions in the book of Revelation. Often passages of poetry are found within a narrative, as when Moses and the Israelites sing to the Lord the beautiful hymn in Exodus 15.

Most poetry has a natural flow and meter; often there is repetition or parallel structure in the verses that requires careful preparation so that the assembly can experience its effect and meaning. Some of the most lovely and memorable phrases from scripture are poetry.

The speaker in a poetic reading is sometimes unnamed, as in the Creation story, but can often be identified. Notice how the prophets are careful to signal when they speak in their own voice and when they speak in the voice of God.

PRAYER: Much of the prayer in scripture is poetic and needs a similar approach for proclamation. Prayer in the Bible is much like prayer in our worship or private lives: it takes on many forms and functions but is generally thanksgiving or intercession prayed by humans to God.

Biblical prayer is seen most frequently in the psalms, the prayers Jesus often prayed. If you are asked to proclaim the psalm at a Mass where there is no cantor to lead the assembly in singing it, remember that the psalm is always addressed to God and always proclaimed with great reverence.

Once you have determined the genre and speaker of the reading, consider the *theme.* Knowing the theme or point of a narrative, discourse, poem, or prayer will allow you to proclaim effectively. For example, when you prepare the proclamation of a narrative with an understanding of the theme of the story, the assembly will hear a cohesive and purposeful reading, rather than a list of seemingly random events.

As previously mentioned, the first reading and Gospel reading will almost certainly be related by theme. The second reading may be related, or may relate better to the previous or subsequent week's second reading. It may be part of a semi-continuous reading of an epistle. But recognizing its theme or identifying a central message will help you to give life and meaning to the reading as you proclaim it. Reference books specifically for lectors will help greatly in this.

Understanding the speaker and theme of the text will lead you to the voice or mood that the text conveys.

Understanding the speaker and theme of the text will lead you to the *voice* or mood that the text conveys. It is important that your proclamation be consistent with this speaker and mood and, therefore, with the theme. For example, the voice you use to proclaim the command from God in the book of Joel to "return to me with your whole heart"[11] will have a different tone than the voice you use to proclaim Paul's charge to the Ephesians to "watch carefully how you live"[12] or the tone you use to proclaim the touching story of the boy Samuel awakening to the presence of God.[13] If you are proclaiming the first reading on the solemnity of the Epiphany of the Lord, a wooden facial expression and monotone voice make no sense as you proclaim, "Rise up in Splendor, Jerusalem! Your light has come, the glory of the Lord shines upon you."[14] The mood of awe and rejoicing that surrounds all the readings for Epiphany absolutely requires an expressive face and voice conveying wonder and joy. A good preparation aid for lectors, biblical commentary, or study Bible can also help you identify genre and theme. These resources often explain how scripture scholars have looked at the text, giving the origins of certain words or explaining certain customs and providing insights and interpretations that may not be familiar to you. Some of these resources can also be quite dense, so if they are helpful, use them, and if not, do not push your preparation to the point of frustration. The resource section beginning on page 62 provides helpful tools for preparation, study, and prayer.

Background and Clarification of a Reading

While you are looking at the theme and genre of a reading and gauging its mood, you will also want to look at the overall context of that piece. Find the reading in the Bible to see what comes before and after. A good study Bible or biblical commentary will shed light on difficult passages. Questions to ask yourself about the overall context of the reading include:

- Who are the main characters and what are their roles? Is there anything we know about particular historical figures that is helpful for understanding this story?

- What is the setting (time and place) of this reading? For example, are the people in Canaan or are they scattered during the Babylonian exile? Is this taking place in the northern or southern kingdom? Is the community addressed in this reading in ancient Israel or Greece? Does the setting give any additional information about what is going on? (Note: An atlas of the Bible is generally inexpensive but can be extremely helpful for a lector to have at home to look up the physical location of a reading and learn something about the lands in the reading.)

• What are the historical events that surround this reading? For example, is this in the time of the ancestors, or the judges, or the kings? (Study Bibles have time lines in their appendices that will help you place the events in the reading you are preparing.)

Looking up the Pronunciation of Words

Before you get much further in your preparation, it is important to identify what words are unfamiliar to you. The names of people and places can be particularly difficult to pronounce, and yet are critical for the assembly to hear correctly in order to understand the reading. There are several good pronunciation guides published in the United States, and it is helpful to have one at home, so that you aren't trying to learn the pronunciation a few minutes before Mass begins.

Names of people and places are critical for the assembly to hear correctly in order to understand the reading.

Incorrect pronunciations can undermine an otherwise fine proclamation. No matter how much authority you give to it, the line is not "A reading from the letter of Saint Paul to the *Philippines*," but rather "A reading from the letter of Saint Paul to the *Philippians*."

Pay particular attention to English words that are easily misread or mispronounced, completely distorting their meaning for the assembly. For example, on the Third Sunday of Advent in Year A, we should not hear from Isaiah: "Here is your God, he comes with *vindiction*"; rather, we should hear "Here is your God, he comes with *vindication*." By mispronouncing *"vindication,"* the assembly is left wondering what that word was and what it means, and they have missed the next sentences about God coming to save us and opening the eyes of the blind. Once you begin the proclamation during Mass, however, read everything with confidence and pronounce words that are repeated in the text consistently so the assembly can follow you.

The Reading in the Context of the Liturgical Season

As previously discussed, each liturgical season has its own sense and flow that is evident in the readings. Reflect on where your reading occurs within the liturgical season or the weeks that have come before and will come after. Is there anything important about where this reading falls for the season, for the community, or even for you personally?

Praying with the Scripture as Preparation

One of the best ways to prepare for your ministry is through prayer. This may seem obvious, but it can sometimes become easy to overlook the importance of praying with the scriptures when you are worried about the mechanics of being a lector. Pope John Paul II reminded us of this in *Dies Domini*: "If Christian individuals and families are not regularly drawing new life from the reading of the sacred text in a spirit of prayer and docility to the church's interpretation, then it is difficult for the liturgical proclamation of the word of God alone to produce the fruit we might expect."[15]

Prayerful preparation also helps us to keep in mind that our Sunday gathering and our ministry within that sacred space is not about us or even about our community, but about God. Our prayer at the Sunday Eucharist is about what God did for us and continues to do for us through Jesus Christ. A prayerful, Christ-centered approach to scripture will come across in your proclamation and will be a great service to the assembly.

Practice Techniques

Once you have identified the theme and genre, looked at the background and context, determined how to pronounce all the words, and prayed with the scripture, practice reading it aloud. What looks easy on the page may sound quite different when you actually speak it.

But first, be sure to "warm up." Just as singers would not open their mouths to sing publicly without first warming up their vocal chords, you should ensure that your voice is warmed up and your throat clear before you approach the ambo. First, take a few moments to open wide and close your mouth several times and move your jaw around. Be sure that you have taken some deep breaths to bring air into your lungs and have practiced controlled exhaling of those breaths with simple vowel sounds. And finally, it is often helpful to drink some water to ensure that there is no phlegm in your throat. These are the tried and true vocal warm ups of international speaking organizations such as Toastmasters International, and they will serve you well to ensure that you do not need to begin by stepping up to the microphone and clearing your throat.[16]

It can be helpful to tape record yourself reading, and to read in front of a mirror. These methods will help you determine whether your voice is portraying the reading well, and whether your facial expressions match your words.

Practice making your volume, pacing, emphasis, and voice quality appropriate for the scripture. The work you have done to thoroughly know and understand this reading should be evident in your voice and face.

It is also helpful to ask someone to listen to you proclaim the reading, and then reflect back to you what they heard in the proclamation. Do they hear what you are trying to convey? Thirty seconds after you *Make your volume, pacing, emphasis, and voice quality appropriate for the scripture.* finish, can they tell you what the reading was about? If so, it is likely that your assembly will also hear what you are conveying. If not, try again.

Over time, practicing again and again will help you to feel more comfortable with each reading and with your role as a lector, and help you to be less self-conscious. If you struggle with "stage fright," practicing regularly will be a great help to you.

Public Speaking Skills to Learn and Practice

The skills that serve public speakers well are the same skills that serve lectors well. These are not easy to master, and indeed people's expectations continue to grow as the many forms of popular media show us so many highly polished presenters.

As lectors we are not expected to be professional actors, but we are expected to take the role seriously and strive to always improve our presentation skills. In this way also, we learn to become more transparent and allow God to be visible in the word. If we mumble or speed through the reading, people will be distracted by us and miss how God is speaking to them. There are five areas in particular to which we should pay close attention in our presentation style.

Control of Breath and Volume

The way we breathe will control the phrasing of the reading and the volume at which it is proclaimed. Keeping our breathing deep and

Breathing should be done in the lungs and not in the head.

steady will also ensure that we stay calmer and more relaxed while we are reading. If you find yourself getting very nervous as you approach the ambo (or think about approaching the ambo), then it is critical that you take a few slow, deep breaths.

Remember that breathing should be done in the lungs and not in the head. This may sound silly, but when you are breathing fast and don't have enough breath to get through a full phrase, you are most likely taking shallow, short breaths. Even while reading, your breaths should fill your lungs so that you have enough air to make it through the phrases of the reading. Breathing at an inopportune time because you are out of air can change the meaning of a phrase. For example, if you are proclaiming the "Song of the Sea" from Exodus 15 during the Easter Vigil, there is a difference in meaning between these two phrasings:

The flood waters covered them, / they sank into the depths [breath]
like a stone. / Your right hand, O LORD, [breath]
magnificent in power, / your right hand [breath]
O LORD, has shattered the enemy.

and

The flood waters covered them, [breath]
    they sank into the depths like a stone. [breath]
Your right hand, O LORD, magnificent in power, [breath]
    your right hand, O LORD, has shattered the enemy.
Exodus 15:5–6

The Lectionary helps us with the phrasing of the readings by breaking them into "sense lines," lines that appear to be in a poetic format and show the reader how passages should be broken into phrases. If you do not have a copy of the Lectionary, a missal, or preparation aid that uses sense lines, you must do the work of breaking the reading into phrasing yourself;[17] otherwise, what you are reading will sound more like a series of strung-together words than phrases that convey meaning. But without proper breath control, it does not matter if you know what the phrases are, you will have a hard time getting through whatever phrases you are using in a reading.

Your breathing will also control the volume of your proclamation. Controlling the volume is not just about using the microphone well or being loud, though both are important. It is also about making sure that you are speaking from the air in your chest, rather than from the air in your nose. This feeling of speaking at a lower part of the body will help you to keep the pitch in a lower and more authoritative part of your voice, and will help you to project your voice, rather than just shout. Shouting is rarely called for in scripture proclamation, but projecting your voice loudly is often appropriate, particularly when there is a great deal of ambient noise in the worship space. Breathing deeply and speaking from your filled lungs will give you the ability to increase the volume, project your voice, and have enough breath to get through full phrases in the reading.

Clear Articulation and Pronunciation

Enunciating words clearly is extremely important for the lector. Make sure that all syllables are pronounced, that the endings of words are not dropped, and that multiple words are not strung together to form one unintelligible word.   *Enunciate!*

This helps the assembly to hear and understand the word of God. Particularly when so many of our communities have a variety of nationalities among both their lectors and assembly members, it is critical for everyone's understanding that there be no mumbling or slurring of words.

We've already discussed the importance of pronouncing words properly. Correct pronunciation allows the assembly to follow the reading and not wonder what it is you really meant to say.

Appropriate Pacing of the Reading

The first principle concerning the pacing of the reading is to slow down. It is rare that a new lector reads too slowly for people to understand the meaning of the text. Reading at a conversational pace is too fast.

While you may feel that you are reading painfully slowly,   *Slow down!*
this will most likely not be the case. Beyond slowing down, the

pace of the reading depends on the text, the space, and the sound system.

Each reading will have points where there should be pauses to emphasize what has just been said. Studying the reading will help you to know where these pauses should go. Likewise, if your passage has any form of litany in it, the reading will dictate if you should speed up a bit in that section to emphasize the litany aspect of the reading or slow down to ensure that people hear each phrase.

Besides understanding the reading and pacing the reading well in its own right, you need to understand the space in which you are proclaiming the reading, and the sound system that you are using. A large church with tile floors will have a delay between the sound made by the lector reading and the sound heard by the people all the way in the back of the church. There may also be an echo. Most churches present some acoustical challenges for the lector. Practicing in the church with the lector trainer will help you determine how long your pauses need to be to allow the words you have spoken to reach everyone. The sound system will also affect this. Some very large churches have two speakers in the front of the church and none anywhere else. Other (mostly newer) churches have installed sound systems that provide almost instantaneous sound to everyone in the church at the same time. Either way, probably there will be an echo that you must let die between paragraphs or individual points in a reading. Again, your trainer will help you master the sound system and the challenges of the building.

Effective Voice Quality and Emphasis

Your preparation of the reading will help you understand the mood and tone of the reading and what needs to be emphasized. What you emphasize in a phrase can potentially change the meaning of that phrase for people hearing it, so the decision should be made carefully. Once you are extremely familiar with the reading and have a good sense of what God is conveying in it, you will be much more comfortable deciding exactly what tone to use and where to place emphasis.

As you consider your voice quality, be careful to keep your voice coming from your lungs and chest, and at a lower, more authoritative tone. Even in readings of great gladness and rejoicing, allowing the pitch of your voice to be high will make it harder for people to hear and understand what you are saying. You can speak in the lower part of your voice with a smile on your face, and the joy will come out in the quality of your vocal expression.

Vocal expression, while extremely helpful in conveying meaning in the reading, can also cross the line from expressive to dramatic and detract from what is being said in favor of calling attention to you, the lector. There is a very thin line between proclaiming scripture and dramatizing scripture. Remember that even when you are reading about the deaths of the brothers in 2 Maccabees on the Thirty-second Sunday in Ordinary Time[18] you are not giving a dramatic reading for a club or a radio show, but are rather conveying the meaning that the King of the world will raise us up to

> *There is a very thin line between proclaiming scripture and dramatizing scripture.*

live again forever. It would be quite easy to make this reading extremely dramatic. The challenge is to make it expressive so that it conveys meaning and is not simply a drama for the sake of drama.

Practicing at Church

A great deal of the preparation we have discussed can be done anywhere. However, it is extremely important, especially as a new lector, that you practice your ministry in the church. This includes practicing everything you will do as a lector from the opening procession through the closing procession.

As with the pacing of the reading, the sound system will make a difference in how the reading comes across. Each sound system is different, and you will need the lector trainer to explain the particulars of your parish system to you. The microphone will either be *omnidirectional* and pick up sound from all sides (in which case it does not need to be moved up or down depending on your height) or *unidirectional* and only pick up that which is spoken directly into it (in which case you will need to move it directly in front of your mouth). The sound system can also help with volume, but you have to learn to project your voice well so that you can truly control the expression of the reading and not simply make it louder or softer.

You will also need to be comfortable with the physical setting of the church. You

> *Practicing all the movements in the lector's routine will make you much less self-conscious and nervous.*

need to know where exactly to sign in when you arrive, where to wait for the opening procession, what path the opening procession will take, where lectors are to sit, and how you are to move to and from the ambo. Practicing the movements around the space—all the movements in the lector's routine—will make you much less self-conscious and nervous.

Most parishes will rehearse all of this with you at least once or twice before you are assigned to be the lector at a Mass. However, if you find that you are not comfortable after those practices, do not be afraid to ask to come back and practice again. In some churches, you will be allowed to come in when it is convenient for you, walk through all the motions in the space, and practice the reading from the ambo, even without someone from the staff present (although the microphone will most likely not be on). Over time, you will begin to feel comfortable with the space, and will be able to focus your energies not on where to go or what to do next, but on proclaiming the scriptures as well as you can.

The Importance of Nonverbal Communication

While we have looked most extensively at the verbal aspects of proclaiming scripture at Mass, your nonverbal communication is also extremely important.

First, it is important to have good posture, whether you are processing or standing at the ambo. Slouching will detract from your reading, as will leaning back and putting your hands in your pockets. Hold

An alert, dignified posture will convey the significance of the proclamation.

your shoulders back, place your legs directly beneath your shoulders (don't lock your knees!), and keep your back straight. This alert, dignified posture will convey the significance of the proclamation. However, take care not to throw your shoulders too far back and your chest too far out so that you project an air of arrogance instead of humility and dignity. Practicing in front of a mirror will help you find the posture that looks and feels appropriate.

While reading from the ambo, it is important to make eye contact with the assembly. The opening line and closing dialogue of the reading can certainly be done while looking at the people. It is also important to look at people during the reading. This really does help to keep people engaged and help to convey meaning. You will feel most comfortable making eye contact throughout the reading if you are familiar enough with it to be able to look up at the people and back down at the Lectionary and not lose your place.

Any gesture that you make should also be done with care and deliberation. The gesture you are most likely to make is bowing, if you pass in front of the altar on your way to or from the ambo (there is no reason to bow if you do not pass in front of the altar). Good liturgical gesture is done with grace and meaning.

> ✠ A deep bow is made to the altar by all who enter the sanctuary (chancel), leave it, or pass before the altar.
>
> —*Ceremonial of Bishops, #72*

In general, hand gestures are not necessary when serving as a lector. So that your hands have a natural place to be, it is a good idea to let them rest on the ambo, holding the Lectionary, or subtly marking your place with a finger.

All of your movements should be done with purpose and reverence, whether walking to or from the ambo, or bowing before the altar. Movements should be neither too fast nor too slow. When standing at the ambo, be still and avoid fidgeting. Shifting your weight back and forth from one foot to the other, or slightly bouncing up and down will distract greatly from your reading. Often these are nervous gestures we are not aware of, so feedback from others is particularly helpful in determining if we have a problem that needs correction.

If you are carrying the Book of the Gospels in the opening procession, or removing the Lectionary after the second reading, it is important that you handle these books reverently. Apart from the readings within them, the books themselves, especially the Book of the Gospels, are symbols of our faith and of the salvation of Christ throughout the history of God's people. They should be carried with two hands and picked up and put down carefully.

Finally, your choice of attire also says something about your ministry and the importance of us gathering in praise and worship of our Lord. Some churches have dress codes for lectors and some do not. If your parish does have a dress code, be sure that you follow it. If not, there are some basic principles that should guide your clothing selections. First, most often you will know when you will be serving as a lector, a leader within the community. Therefore, you should be dressed in such a way as to convey that you both knew you were coming to serve, and cared about that service to the people and to God. In this case, blue jeans, shorts, or T-shirts are inappropriate attire. Second, your clothing should never distract from your ministry. If you have bare shoulders, a bare midriff, too low of a neckline, tight clothing, or colors

In matters of attire, simplicity, modesty, and dignity are your goals.

far brighter than is customary for your community, most people in the assembly will spend more energy looking at you than listening to the reading. This takes away from all the preparation you have put into your ministry and makes it difficult for people to hear the word of God from you. Distraction of this kind is easily avoided and should be. Give some thought to what clothes in your wardrobe would be most appropriate, keeping in mind that simplicity, modesty, and dignity are your goals.

Reflection and Self-Evaluation

As important as it is to prepare well for proclaiming the sacred scripture, it is equally important to reflect on your proclamation immediately afterward to evaluate how well you are doing in your ministry. Neither preparation nor reflection is effective without the other. During your service as a lector over the coming years, you will find that if you are to serve the assembly well and continue to grow in your ministry, neither can be eliminated—even if you are tempted to think you know what you're doing and have done it all before. Use the Questions for Self-Evaluation to guide you in this process.

Questions for Self-Evaluation

1. Did I feel prepared and ready to serve the community?

_____

_____

_____

_____

_____

2. Did I understand my reading and have a sense of the theme I was conveying to the assembly?

_____

_____

_____

_____

_____

3. Were there areas of the reading where I stumbled? If so, do I know why?

_____

_____

_____

_____

_____

4. What did I feel good about that I would like to be sure to remember in the future?

_____

_____

_____

_____

_____

5. Do I have a sense that I ministered to the community well, and can do so again in the future?

_____

_____

_____

_____

_____

Even more helpful is the practice of group feedback with other lectors that should be a part of all of our ministries. These sessions should occur regularly, perhaps monthly or bimonthly, so that the work of the lector and the appropriate feedback is not forgotten over a span of several months' time.

It can seem quite daunting to present yourself to a group for their reactions to work you care about. But honest feedback is one of the best means we have of learning and growing in our ministry. Group feedback sessions with other lectors allow people to say to one another, "This is how you helped me to understand what you were proclaiming, and this is what got in the way." Group feedback also helps us gauge the line between the expressive proclamation we are called to give, and dramatization of the reading that is not appropriate. Without input from

Honest feedback is one of the best means we have of learning and growing in our ministry.

others, it is hard to know how well God's word is truly being received by the assembly. And when we take the time to critically listen to others and participate in their reflection processes, we can pick up on the good characteristics of their proclamation styles and learn from their mistakes as well as our own.

When engaging in a group feedback process, it is most helpful for participants to speak as members of the assembly about what helped or hindered their experience of the reading, rather than trying to take the role of a teacher. It is also helpful to distinguish between the clarity and effectiveness of proclamation and one's personal taste. For example, telling a fellow lector that his or her level of drama made you uncomfortable is appropriate for the group process, but critiquing the theme that the lector chose to emphasize, simply because you would have chosen another theme, is less helpful. Telling a fellow lector that his or her attire distracted you from hearing the scripture is appropriate, but complaining about colors you don't care for is not. The Questions for a Group Feedback Session will help focus the exercise.

Questions for a Group Feedback Session

1. Was the lector's voice loud enough? Did the phrasing of the reading make sense?

_____

_____

_____

_____

2. Did the lector articulate the words well or were some of them slurred or mumbled? Were words pronounced correctly?

_____

_____

_____

_____

3. Did the pace allow people to listen and follow?

_____

_____

_____

_____

4. Did the quality of voice match the mood of the reading?

_____

_____

_____

_____

_____

5. Was the nonverbal communication helpful or distracting? Was the posture good? Did the lector look at the assembly? Was the movement of the lector graceful? Did the lector's attire distract from the reading?

_____

_____

_____

_____

_____

Overall, if lectors gather together and are open to the process of feedback, it will help all of them to grow in their ministry and in their understanding of the impact of their ministry on others. This is a tremendous gift!

Frequently Asked Questions

1. What should I do if I make a mistake such as misspeaking a word or an entire line?

While good preparation helps us to cut down on errors, almost all lectors have the experience of making a mistake at some point. If you realize the mistake immediately, it is generally best to pause slightly, and then restate the proper word or line and go forward. It is never a good idea, however, to remark on or apologize for the error ("Oh, wait" or "I'm sorry") and then fix what you've said. If you simply correct the error and move on, people will understand and will remain focused on the text you are proclaiming, rather than on the fact that a mistake was made. If you are most of the way through the text or at the end, and realize a mistake was made, let it go.

No matter what happens, do not let a mistake at one point in the reading distract you from doing your best with the remainder of the reading. Taking a deep breath, focusing on where you are, and continuing to proclaim the reading well is the best way to "correct" any errors. Remembering also that most people will not recognize the mistake, and will simply listen to what you are proclaiming, can be very reassuring.

2. Our parish does not have a Book of the Gospels. Should we carry the Lectionary in the opening procession?

No. If your parish does not have a Book of the Gospels, then no book is carried in the opening procession. In the same way, if there is no Book of the Gospels, the Gospel reader (deacon or priest) will bow to the altar in prayer, and then process to the ambo during the Gospel acclamation, without incense, candles, or servers.

3. How should the Book of the Gospels be placed on the altar?

The Book of the Gospels is often richly decorated and very expensive. We reverence the Book of the Gospels by carrying it in procession, placing it on the altar, and processing it to the ambo for the proclamation of the Gospel. It is not necessary or advisable to give reverence to the book by standing it up, open, on the altar. Over time, this will pull the pages out of the binding and ruin a book that should last the church several generations. It is acceptable and correct to simply lay the book flat on the altar.

4. What if I am reading both the first and second reading? Should I stay at the ambo during the responsorial psalm or return to my seat?

Once a reading is finished, it is best to return to your seat, even if you are also doing the next reading. In many parishes, the cantor will come to the ambo to lead the psalm. Even if this is not the case for your parish, one of our roles as ministers is to help the assembly focus its attention on the center of the liturgy, and if you are not reading the psalm, you should be seated so that all can focus on the psalm rather than wonder why you are still at the ambo.

However, if you are reading both the first reading and the psalm, you should stay at the ambo, pause for at least 15 to 20 seconds, and then begin the psalm, rather than moving back and forth.

5. Should I genuflect when I pass the tabernacle on my way to or from the ambo?

No. When the tabernacle is located in the sanctuary, the priest, deacon, and other ministers genuflect when they approach the altar (opening procession) and when they depart (closing procession), "but not during the celebration of Mass itself."[19] Indeed, moving to and from the ambo is a processional movement, and we do not genuflect in processions during the Mass.[20] The *Ceremonial of Bishops* states that "a deep bow is made to the altar by all who enter the sanctuary (chancel), leave it, or *pass before the altar*" (emphasis added).[21]

6. I understand that there is a three-year cycle of readings for Sundays. Why do I hear the same readings during Lent each year?

During the Third, Fourth, and Fifth Sundays of Lent, many parishes will use the readings of Year A each year. This is appropriate when there are members of the elect preparing for Baptism at the Easter Vigil. The readings of Year A are the basis for the "scrutinies" that the members of the elect undergo during these weeks. "The scrutinies are meant to uncover, then heal all that is weak, defective, or sinful in the hearts of the elect; to bring out, then strengthen all that is upright, strong, and good."[22]

7. What if I am assigned a reading that I am simply unable to proclaim well?

When you first know when you are scheduled to read, you should look at the readings you are assigned and come to some understanding of them. While some readings may be difficult to understand, complicated in their theology, or may be a "hard teaching" with which you are struggling, as lectors we should be willing to take on the challenge of spending time with those pieces and coming to an understanding of the text that we can express.

A reader will occasionally, though not very often, have difficulty publicly proclaiming a reading. If you pray with a reading and find that you just cannot proclaim it with meaning, let the coordinator of lectors know, and find a substitute. However, this should be a personal call for you to spend more time with that reading and its context so that you can minister well the next time you are called on to read it.

8. What if I walk into church and am asked to fill in for a lector at that Mass?

Certainly lectors always try to be as prepared as possible. But occasionally the unexpected intervenes and you may be asked to read at a Mass when you did not expect it. Obviously, the vast majority of the preparation cannot be done in this case. Your regular preparation for Mass as a member of the assembly should include reading the scriptures before coming to Mass so that you will already have some familiarity with them. Whether or not that is the case, you can still take a prayerful moment to read through the passage before Mass and at least gain a basic sense of what you will be proclaiming. And if you are certain that you absolutely cannot do a decent job of proclaiming the scripture in this situation, than you need to tell the priest celebrant or liturgy coordinator, and ask that they find someone else to fill in.

9. What if my reading is not in the Lectionary or what if I need a larger size type than is in the Lectionary?

For a variety of reasons, there may be times when your reading will need to be paper clipped into the Lectionary or Book of the Gospels. This should be done before the Mass, with a plastic paper clip or two that will not damage any edging of the pages. The page marker should be placed at this spot and the book opened and read as usual. The pages should not draw any special attention to themselves. At no time should you simply carry a piece of paper to the ambo to read from, nor should you pull one from your pocket and unfold it. To the assembly, the reading should appear as though from the book.

Responding to Difficult or Unusual Situations

No matter how well prepared you are for your ministry, every now and then something out of the ordinary will happen. The first principle for all ministers is to stay calm. The most outrageous situations are easier for the entire assembly to deal with if those they perceive as leaders (including you as a lector) remain calm and composed and keep a sense of reverence about what they are doing. It is also especially important that we always exhibit a sense of hospitality and charity. This is sometimes easier said than done, but is important to keep in mind.

Listed below are some of the more likely difficult or unusual situations to come up. It is by no means an exhaustive list, because if we knew everything that was going to happen, we wouldn't be surprised by it. These examples will give you a few principles for making wise decisions on how to deal with events in the immediacy of the moment. We always pray that the Spirit will be with us in such moments, leading us to respond in the most loving and helpful ways.

Noisy Children

Children and noise are, thankfully, a part of most of our assemblies. They remind us of young life and hope that is constantly growing in our communities. When you are trying to proclaim scripture, however, they can sometimes be distracting for both you and the assembly. It is occasionally helpful to pause for a moment and allow excess noise to die down, particularly before you begin a reading. When this does not work, it may become necessary to project your voice slightly more forcefully in the microphone. If this is not enough, then you must simply go on as best you can.

There are a few times a year when we know in advance that the church is going to be especially loud: Christmas and Easter. On these occasions when there are many visitors and a larger than usual assembly, it is a good idea to have a special rehearsal to prepare lectors for the higher noise level. At that time, all the lectors would gather and practice their readings from the ambo, with the sound system on, while the other lectors make lots of noise in the church. This will allow the liturgy coordinator to set the microphone levels at a slightly higher than normal volume if possible, and will allow you to be prepared to proclaim the scripture well, without being distracted by the extra noise around you.

Someone Takes Your Seat while You Are Reading

Many lectors have had the experience of getting up to read and finding that their seat has been taken quietly by a latecomer. If your parish has a good group of ushers, this is less likely to happen. If you don't have ushers, you could put a small "reserved" sign on your seat. But if it does happen and you can see that there is no space for you as you leave the ambo, you should go to the side or back of the church rather than returning to your seat.

Distracting or Alarming Interruptions

If you are in the middle of a reading and there is a sudden loud noise from outside the building (such as sirens passing by), it is generally helpful to pause for a few seconds and then resume where you stopped, as long as this will not interrupt a sentence or phrase. If it would be an awkward place to pause, then getting louder for a few moments during the distraction and lowering your voice again once it passes would be the best course of action.

Every now and then there will be a sudden commotion in the church. Standing at the ambo, you may notice it, even though the majority of the assembly does not. If it is a small commotion in one area, then it is best to simply continue with the reading. If, however, someone yells for help and everyone turns to see what is going on, the priest celebrant should attend to what is happening and you should wait for him to tell you that it is time to continue. At that point it is usually best to begin the reading from the beginning.

Questions for Reflection and Discussion

1. What about the liturgy and scriptures draws you toward serving as lector? Have you found a particular love for the scriptures over time or recently? How do you hope to share that love for the scriptures with others through your ministry?

_____

_____

_____

_____

_____

_____

2. How do you hope to personally grow and develop in your faith through this ministry?

_____

_____

_____

_____

_____

3. Are there any lectors who you have found particularly effective in their proclamation? What is it about their ministry that touches you? What skills of theirs do you wish to emulate in your own ministry?

_____

_____

_____

_____

_____

4. As you begin your ministry, what study and preparation can you commit yourself to on a regular basis?

_____

_____

_____

_____

_____

NOTES

1. GIRM, #101.

2. Luke 2:1.

3. In some areas, the lector may be seated in the sanctuary. It is best to consult your pastoral leadership staff or Office for Divine Worship to determine local practice. If the lectors are seated in the sanctuary, then they will join in the closing procession. If the lectors return to their pew, they will not join in the closing procession.

4. GIRM, #56.

5. GIRM, #61.

6. GIRM, #39.

7. GIRM, #71.

8. Ibid.

9. GIRM, #69.

10. Rule of Saint Benedict, #38.

11. Ash Wednesday, Lectionary #219.

12. Twentieth Sunday in Ordinary Time, Year B, Lectionary #119.

13. Second Sunday in Ordinary Time, Year B, Lectionary #65.

14. Lectionary, #20.

15. *Dies Domini*, #40.

16. These vocal techniques were adapted from Toastmasters International. Please refer to their Web site for additional information: www.toastmasters.org.

17. *Workbook for Lectors and Gospel Readers* is a very helpful resource for this task. See page 64 of the resource section.

18. Year C, Lectionary #156.

19. GIRM, #274.

20. GIRM, #274.

21. CB, #72.

22. *Rite of Christian Initiation of Adults*, #141.

Resources

Lector Preparation

The Catholic Bible, Personal Study Edition: New American Bible. Jean Marie Heisberger, general editor. New York, New York: Oxford University Press, 1995.

    This is a terrific resource for anyone who is beginning to study the scriptures. Resources include a reading guide, discussion questions, background essays on aspects of Bible study, a glossary of specialized terms, full-color New Oxford Bible maps, and more. For the purposes of personally praying with, studying, and reflecting on the scriptures, this is an excellent resource for all lectors.

The Catholic Study Bible: Second Edition. Donald Senior and John J. Collins, editor. New York, New York: Oxford University Press, 2006.

    For those who have already spent some time studying the scriptures, this study Bible will provide more depth. Readers will benefit from commentary regarding the historical, literary, and theological dimensions of scripture. This Bible also includes an extensive Reading Guide, helpful marginal references, and full-color maps.

Anchor Bible Dictionary. Des Moines, Iowa: Anchor Bible, 1992.

    This dictionary provides background information on people, places, and events in the Bible. You can get a quick overview of the book you are reading, and explanations of unfamiliar rituals or celebrations that are in your text. This is a very readable and accessible preparation resource.

New Jerome Biblical Commentary. Upper Saddle River, New Jersey: Prentice Hall, 1989.

    The *New Jerome Biblical Commentary* is a line-by-line commentary on the scriptures by Catholic biblical scholars. This reference is not an easy read, but it can explain many details in the content and context of the reading.

Lectionary for Mass Sundays, Solemnities, Feasts f the Lord and the Saints: Study Edition. Chicago, Illinois: Liturgy Training Publications, 1999.

This convenient and comprehensive paperback volume contains all of the readings for the Sundays of Years A, B, and C and those for solemnities and feast days. All scripture texts are from the *Revised New American Bible* (RNAB) approved for use in the United States of America. The introduction explains the role of scripture in the Mass and how readings have been selected—illuminating information for lectors!

Guide to the Revised Lectionary. Connell, Martin. Chicago, Illinois: Liturgy Training Publications, 1998.

It is important for lectors to have an understanding of the Lectionary. This book helps to answer questions about the revised Roman Catholic Lectionary: its origins and history, how scripture is organized, what is left out of the Lectionary, and more.

The Weekday Lectionary: Study Edition. Chicago, Illinois: Liturgy Training Publications, 2002.

This convenient and comprehensive paperback volume contains all of the readings for Weekday Masses, which are from the *Revised New American Bible* approved for use in the United States.

Pronunciation Guide to the Sunday Lectionary. Meyers, Susan E. Chicago, Illinois: Liturgy Training Publications, 1999.

This is a straightforward little pronunciation guide that lectors should have at home when they are preparing for their ministry. Any words that appear in the Sunday Lectionary and have questionable or difficult pronunciations are included.

Rosser, OSB, Aelred. *A Well-Trained Tongue: Formation in the Ministry of Reader.* Chicago, Illinois: Liturgy Training Publications, 1996.

This is a helpful guide for both beginning and veteran lectors. For group formation, one-on-one, or individual study. Filled with practical exercises to help the reader develop the skills needed for the more challenging passages in the Lectionary. Inviting discussions include: the literary genres of the Bible, the liturgical year, the three-year structure of the Lectionary, what the reader might wear for this ministry, their place in the procession and how a formation team might be formed in the parish.

Sommers, Audrey. *Lector and Gospel Reader Workshop: A Resource for Bringing God's Word to Life.* Chicago, Illinois: Liturgy Training Publications, 2006.

This resource is an interactive workshop on DVD for lectors and their trainers. The workshop combines the liturgical and spiritual aspects of being an effective lector with public speaking techniques. It addresses the role of the lector according to the Second Vatican Council and provides the latest information on the *General Instruction of the Roman Missal.* Participants will learn breathing techniques and will recite scriptural tongue twisters and word emphasis exercises before proclaiming a reading on camera for group critiques. The kit contains all instruction, promotion, and marketing materials needed in electronic form for a parish to have a successful workshop. It also provides prayers and valuable handouts for home study.

Workbook for Lectors and Gospel Readers. Chicago, Illinois: Liturgy Training Publications.

An essential week-by-week preparation tool for lectors, this fundamental annual resource is also helpful for presiders and lectors, homilists, and those who prepare the liturgy. A copy given to each lector and Gospel reader promotes good proclamation and love of scripture in the Sunday assembly. Readings are presented in sense line format—as they appear in the Lectionary—to aid the reader in preparation, and Lectionary numbers are included for each set of readings. The author offers helpful commentaries for each reading, providing background information and tips for effective proclamation. Margin notes point out logical divisions in the passages and help the reader with difficult pronunciations. Words are marked in the reading to aid the reader in stressing important sections and concepts. Two editions are printed each year: one for churches in the United States with the NAB translation of scripture and another for churches in Canada with the NRSV translation of scripture.

General Instruction of the Roman Missal. Congregation for Divine Worship and the Discipline of the Sacraments. Washington, D.C.: United States Conference of Catholic Bishops, Inc., 2003.

    The GIRM is the definitive document on the theology of the liturgy and the way that the liturgy is celebrated. All who serve as ministers at the liturgy can gain further insight into their role and ministry by reading and reflecting on the liturgy as a whole. Also available from LTP in the *Liturgy Documents, Volume 1, Fourth Edition.*

Turner, Paul. *Guide to the General Instruction of the Roman Missal.* Chicago, Illinois: Liturgy Training Publications, 2003.

    This brief, accessible guidebook offers priests and parish ministers a straightforward commentary on the *General Instruction of the Roman Missal.* Working from the Latin text, Turner highlights three important principles: the sacrifice of Christ, the holiness of the Eucharist, and the participation of the ministers. This helpful resource is a must for anyone who prepares the liturgy for a parish assembly. Also available in Spanish.

Wood, Geoff. *Living the Lectionary.* Chicago, Illinois: Liturgy Training Publications.

    A separate volume is available for Years A, B, and C.

    Geoff Wood's reflections on the Sunday readings make visible scripture's perennial applicability to human experience. Through reference to Western literature as well as his life experiences, he engages our imagination and helps us to see the wisdom of the biblical word shine forth.

Liturgical and Daily Mass Reading Reference. Chicago, Illinois: Liturgy Training Publications.

    This handy booklet is published annually to give the Mass readings for each day of the year.

Resources for Prayer and Reflection

At Home with the Word. Chicago, Illinois: Liturgy Training Publications.

    Prepare to listen to God's word each Sunday, at home alone or with a group. It contains the texts of the Sunday readings for the particular year (Year A, B, or C), the responsorial psalms, and scripture reflections with questions for study and discussion, as well as meditations on the practice of virtue. It uses the NAB scripture texts from the *Lectionary for Mass* for the United States and is also available in large print and in a Spanish-language version titled *Palabra de Dios*.

Daily Prayer. Chicago, Illinois: Liturgy Training Publications.

This annual resource provides an order of prayer for each day of the liturgical year. Using a familiar order of prayer, it enables further reflection on the sacred mysteries celebrated in the liturgy. The Gospel of the day from the daily Mass is provided, and the prayer texts and reflections are in tune with the observance of the seasons, solemnities, feasts of the Lord, and commemoration of saints celebrated during the liturgical year.

Praying the Bible: An Introduction to Lectio Divina, by Mariano Magrassi, OSB, translated by Edward Hagman, OFM CAP. Collegeville, Minnesota: The Liturgical Press, 1998.

The author begins with the proclamation of scripture in the liturgy, showing how private prayerful reading of scripture *(lectio divina)* and communal prayerful hearing of scripture are two inseparable practices that nourish each other. Providing rich insights from early Church writers on the role of scripture in the spiritual life as well as their advice on developing the disposition for *lectio divina,* this book offers an inspiring and fortifying initiation into an ancient practice that will be especially helpful for lectors.

Web Sites

New American Bible: www.usccb.org/nab/

The Web site of the United States Conference of Catholic Bishops has a section where you can click a date on the calendar for the next two months, and it will give you the readings of the day. This is particularly helpful if you don't have a printed listing of the readings.

Toastmasters International: http://www.toastmasters.org/

This Web site is a helpful resource for improving public speaking. It provides support, skills, and techniques for effective oral communication.

Spanish Resources

Manual para proclamadores de la palabra—Estados Unidos. Chicago, Illinois: Liturgy Training Publications.

Similar to *Workbook for Lectors and Gospel Readers,* this annual contains the Lectionary texts for Sundays and major feast days. The scripture translations are used from the *Leccionario Mexicano* and the *Leccionario Hispanoamericano.* Margin notes are included to provide a context for the readings.

Palabra de Dios. Chicago, Illinois: Liturgy Training Publications.

Written especially for Spanish-speaking communities in the United States, this annual publication includes the Sunday scripture readings as found in the Mexican Lectionary, a reflection on one of the readings for study or discussion, and questions to stimulate and guide the user. Each week, the section called "Viviendo nuestra fe" gives suggestions for daily living. You also will find the citations of weekday readings and those for special feast days, along with simple orders of Morning, Evening, and Night Prayer.

Glossary

AMBO: A dignified and stationary place from which the readings, responsorial psalm, and Easter proclamation are to be proclaimed. It may also be used for giving the homily and for announcing the intentions of the Prayer of the Faithful.

BOOK OF THE GOSPELS: The collection of Gospel passages that may occur on Sundays or other major occasions, including solemnities, feasts of the Lord, and ritual Masses.

DISCOURSE: A speech, lecture, or letter which makes an argument or explanation.

GENRES: Literary types that have a characteristic style, form, and subject matter.

LECTIO DIVINA: a process of slow meditation on the word of God.

LECTIONARY: A four-volume series that contains the readings for Sundays, weekdays, and various needs and occasions.

LECTOR: Any lay minister who reads from the Lectionary at Mass (also called a reader).

LITURGY OF THE EUCHARIST: Begins with the Preparation of the Gifts and ends with the Prayer after Communion, during which the action of the Mass is centered around the altar.

LITURGY OF THE WORD: The parts of Mass from the first reading through the Prayer of the Faithful during which the action of the Mass is centered around the ambo.

NARRATIVE: A story.

PROCLAMATION: The act of proclaiming, that is, the act of making known publicly. Within the context of the role of the lector, proclamation is the act of making known to the gathered assembly "the continuity of the work of salvation according to God's wonderful plan."[1]

PROFOUND BOW: A gesture that "signifies reverence and honor shown to the persons themselves or to the signs that represent them."[2] A profound bow is generally made from the waist. In the liturgy, profound bows are made by the celebrant to the altar, during the prayer *Munda cor meum* ("Almighty God, cleanse my heart . . .") and *In spiritu humilitatis* ("Lord God, we ask you to receive . . ."), in the Creed at the words *Et incarnatus est* ("by the power of the Holy Spirit . . . and became man"—in this instance, *all* bow), and in the Roman Canon at the words *Supplices te rogamus* ("Almighty God, we pray that your angel . . ."). The same kind of bow is made by the deacon when he asks for a blessing before the proclamation of the Gospel. In addition, the priest bows slightly as he speaks the words of the Lord at the consecration.[3]

THEME: A topic or subject matter.

NOTES

1. GIRM, #357.

2. GIRM, #275.

3. GIRM, #275b.

Prayer of Preparation:
Saint Patrick's Breastplate

Christ with me, Christ before me, Christ behind me,
Christ in me, Christ beneath me, Christ above me,
Christ on my right, Christ on my left,
Christ when I lie down, Christ when I sit down, Christ
when I arise,
Christ in the heart of every man who thinks of me,
Christ in the mouth of every one who speaks of me,
Christ in every eye that sees me,
Christ in every ear that hears me.